anyone...especially the artists out there who need to know how truly divine they really are."

Jenny Gould,
Dancer, Choreographer, Writer

"*Wired for Creativity* truly describes Candace Long, for she is one of the most creative people I have ever known. She's been through the fire and emerged triumphant with a powerful story to tell. I believe this book will be used to set many others free to understand the gifts God gave them to better our world."

Glenda Anderson
Co-Founder, Paul Anderson Youth Home

"Candace has always given glory to God. Now, with the stroke of her pen, she has the opportunity to touch many lives to light the pathway for other creatives."

Joe Loesch
President, Creative License, Inc. – Nashville, TN
Author, Bible Stories for Kids

"*Wired For Creativity* has greatly impacted my life and set me free as a creative. I now have two new streams of income using multiple talents whereas before I had a very unclear understanding of the gifts I was given. I strongly believe that this book will unlock the doors for many creatives as it has for me."

D'Ann Medlin
Designer, Painter, Illustrator

"I was overwhelmed with Candace's material, not expecting it to relate to people in the business world like me. It gave me a much clearer understanding of working with creative people. This book is for everyone!"

Jim Medlin
President, Beacon Building Consultants

Go forth in your
creative gifting!
Candace Long

WIRED
for
Creativity

Candace Long

E∥ergreen
PRESS

Wired for Creativity
by Candace Long

ISBN 1-58169-158-0
For Worldwide Distribution
Printed in the U.S.A.

Evergreen Press
P.O. Box 191540 • Mobile, AL 36619
800-367-8203

TABLE OF CONTENTS

Acknowledgments

There are many people to thank, for without them this book would never have been birthed. I am thankful first to God for the creative gifts He's given me and for His patience when I refused to leave Him alone until He gave me the answers I was seeking. I thank my dear friends who have accompanied me, encouraged me, and mentored me on this journey: Glenda Anderson, Janet & Allen Broughton, Bob Dorsey, Mariette Edwards, Mimi & Alan Gould, Neal Hughs, D'Ann & Jim Medlin, Ted Moore, Marie Morton, Connie Parks, Brenda Pauley, JoAnn Pflug, Mike Ring, Stan Roberson, Tim Thomas, Sarah Tinnon, and David West.

I want to thank my Evergreen literary family—fellow creatives indeed—whose gifts helped flesh out my manuscript: consultant Keith Carroll, editor Kathy Banashak, and publisher Brian Banashak.

Special thanks to my father, Charles Lowe, who encouraged me long ago to pursue my dreams, saying, "The best investment you can make is in yourself." And finally, I thank my precious son Tyler, who has given me the freedom to be who I am—though I'm sure he often questions why in the world he was given a creative for a mother!

Introduction

WIRED FOR CREATIVITY is a personal journey that uncovered two life-changing truths written thousands of years ago: first, that we were created and wired to be creative; and secondly, we were each created for a unique and distinct purpose.

I wrote it for two groups of people. First, it's written for my group—I call us "creatives"—those who know we are wired differently. We are a unique breed of people who go through life feeling we don't fit in anywhere. The book pinpoints the nine distinguishing marks of a creative. It also explains our unique journey and why we often find ourselves struggling with defeat, discouragement, and financial hardship.

It is also written for people who have never thought of themselves as particularly creative, but they'd like to learn more about it and expand their own creative potential. My goal is to provide some mental handles for embracing a supernatural ability that has been available to everyone since the beginning of time. I have not received a Ph.D. in creativity. Rather, I am simply one who, for over 30 years, has experienced countless manifestations of creativity in the business, music, artistic, and entertainment arenas.

Creativity comes from our Creator. It's part of the divine DNA He gave each one of us. In fact, we are "wired" to be able to hear and receive inspiration, ideas, illumination, solutions, concepts, music, art, and theories. It's true that some are more wired than others, but the good news is, we can grow in the gifting. It's an ability the world needs most desperately now, as we face crises such as immorality, terrorism, economic instability, and epidemic diseases, just to name a few. We *need* creative solutions. I believe the Creator has these solutions and desires to give them to us.

Just what is creativity, and how can we use it to change our world? It all starts with you, and your individual grasp of your God-given potential.

ARE YOU A CREATIVE?

Answer the following questions. *(The more "yes" answers, the more you are naturally "wired.")*

1. Do you have emotional highs and lows?

2. Do you feel you were created for a purpose, but don't know what it is?

3. Have you experienced unusual or "supernatural" revelation of ideas, music, art, etc?

4. Do you often feel different from others, like you don't fit in?

5. Are you sensitive toward other people or situations?

6. Have you experienced vivid dreams or visions?

7. Have you ever seen trends (songs, ideas, art, etc.) that are now the latest "craze" only to realize you had those same ideas years ago?

8. Is your mind often churning with so many ideas that you don't know what to do first?

9. Have you experienced blocks, setbacks, and disappointments when trying to pursue your passion?

10. Are you drawn to spiritual things?

CHAPTER 1

In the Beginning... *Creativity*

C reatives have been called many things over the years—
weirdos, long-hairs, rebels, eclectics, non-conformists,
loners, dreamers, and even geniuses. When we creatives
told our parents what we wanted to do with our lives, we often
heard, "That's just a hobby. Go get a real job!" We attend our class
reunions and shudder when we hear classmates discuss their
Junior League stints, or who has just been named president of a
Fortune 500 company or married one. With shame we compare
ourselves with peers who are now respected bankers, engineers,
doctors, or entrepreneurs. When the attention turns to us and we
say, "Well, I've been researching a screenplay for the last five
years," they reply, "Really? Who do you work for, Paramount?"
When our response is, "No, but I'm getting ready to submit it to
them," we receive the all-too-familiar look accompanied by the following unspoken thoughts: *Doing all this work for no money...one
of those dreamers. Totally out of touch. Never make anything out
of herself.*

I have periodically grappled with questions about being creative: Why am I different from other people? Why do some people
have more creativity than others? Where does it come from? Can
we get more? Why are some people creatively more successful than
others? Why does the Bible say, "Many are called, but few are
chosen"? Does that saying apply to those in the creative arts?

I recall attending a music conference prior to the "mother-of-
all-music-festivals," Explo '72 in Dallas, Texas, where I was one of
the performers. Composer/arranger Paul Johnson was speaking to
some of the most well-known Christian music groups in the
country. Already sensing that my destiny had something to do with
music, my ears perked up when he made the perplexing statement,

"Many believe they are called...but only a few are chosen. There are too many Ishmaels in the Christian music industry...not enough Isaacs." He was exhorting us to examine ourselves and determine if God had truly called us into this work, or if we just wanted to be in the business, hoping to find some measure of self-glory. I became troubled, and began to ask myself over the years, "Are you *sure* God is calling you to do this?" After all, I certainly wanted to be in the center of God's will and not an Ishmael!

I have struggled all my life trying to understand what it means to be a "creative." I use the word "creative" as a noun rather than as an adjective for a very simple reason: there are certain people like me who function totally in the creative arena, meaning they make their living at and through their creativity. Not too many years ago, I went to my trusted therapist (who helped me weather many a storm), and with tears streaming down my face, asked the most sincere, gut-wrenching question I knew how to ask, "How are creatives supposed to live in this world?"

For most of us the struggle is intense because the truth is that we're different. We don't fit in. During college, I went to fraternity parties with my friends and always left filled with self-recrimination because I couldn't stand them. Everybody else was having a good time, why couldn't I? There had to be something wrong with me. It took years to understand that my "differentness" was nothing to be ashamed of, but rather to be embraced. It was during those miserable years (the bulk of my life) that I was book-ended by feelings of shame and self-affirmation.

I have spent countless years trying to understand just what creativity is, and to train myself in it. At any given time if I were called upon to come up with some creative idea—a song, a film, a book, a marketing slogan—or formulate a business solution, I have always been able to produce. I never had to wait for some mystical moment when the inspiration would hit. For me, the inspiration has always been there, but my challenge was learning how to consistently tap into it.

Creativity is not an ability for which I take credit; I have long understood that this quality belongs to the divine arena and is bestowed as a gift or a blessing. I remember once many years ago someone asked me, "What would you most like to be known for?" After some thought, I replied, "I would like to be known as someone who was trusted and respected to come forth with whatever was needed in any given area. If Stephen Spielberg needed a hit song for the closing credits of his next film, he would call me. If NBC were looking for a hit TV series, they would take my call and read my latest project. If Hallmark were searching for a brilliant new marketing campaign or product line, my card would be in their rolodex."

I am a generalist, a creative problem-solver who applies the creative gifting to whatever medium in which I am currently working. Because I have continually stretched my own creative envelope, I view creativity with complete awe. It is a gift the world needs most desperately now, as we face countless crises and challenges: immorality, ethical chaos, global terrorism, wars, economic instability, epidemic diseases, overpopulation, and poverty, just to name a few. As a world, we need creative solutions.

I believe the Creator has these solutions. Furthermore, I believe He desires to gift His children with world-changing and wealth-producing blessings so we can be better stewards of those things most on His heart and fulfill the purposes for which we were created. We are approaching a time in history like no other, when a great wave of creativity is building in the heavens, ready to be released. Will we catch it? Will we be found worthy as a generation to receive the inspiration and the ideas that will better our world? Or will God find a people glued to their remotes or their favorite website, receiving data from transmitted sources other than the Divine? Just what is creativity, and how can we use it to change our world?

UNDERSTANDING CREATIVE TEMPERAMENTS

I stumbled onto the beginnings of understanding being a creative through a client of mine that regularly utilized the Myers-Briggs personality type testing in their personnel interviews. One day I took it just for fun. Through it I learned that most creatives (writers, musicians, artists, dancers, performers, sculptors) fall into the NF temperament (Intuitive-Feeling), which is one of four basic personality temperaments according to Jungian theory. What became more enlightening to me, however, is that this group is a far cry from composing 25% of the population! On the contrary, extroverted NFs make up only 5% of the world's population, whereas introverted NFs like me make up only 1% of them. No wonder I had felt different all my life! I also began to understand that the central core need of NFs is to find their meaning and purpose in life. That idea certainly resonated with me because over the years I often was depressed, thinking I had missed my purpose, only to begin the search all over again. As Keirsay and Bates explain in their classic book, *Please Understand Me*, it is the NFs "restless search of self" that runs throughout his/her life.[1]

Other personality types began to interact with my findings, and something resonated about creativity with them as well. I recall the first Creativity Training Workshop I held to try out my material for the masses, so to speak. One man who had never thought of himself as creative stood up at the end during our feedback time, and with tears running down his cheeks he remarked, "I don't know when I have ever been so personally inspired. This workshop really spoke to me." I suddenly saw a bigger picture and began to understand that creativity is not merely limited to those few who try to earn their living through it. Rather, it is that divine quality which separates us from the animal kingdom…that mysterious essence given to everyone by the Creator, in varying degrees.

In the mid 70s, I had a performance scheduled in Nashville. I was fronting for well-known author Ann Kiemel and knew that one or two record producers would be in the audience, coming specifically to hear me. Pretty heady stuff. I decided, therefore, that rather than do the traditional intro of Ann after my show, I would write a song about her by way of introduction. I thought it a brilliant idea. The song was cleverly written, since I had researched all about Ms. Kiemel. I had the audience in the palm of my hand. At the end of the song I said, "Ladies and gentlemen, Miss Ann Kiemel." The audience went wild.

Following the performance, many flocked to say how much they enjoyed my show. I remember three young teenage girls in particular, saying, "You were wonderful. You are so talented." I basked in their adoration. A couple of years later, I realized that one of those girls was a very young Amy Grant. Imagine my reaction watching her career rise to stardom while mine shrank into oblivion. For more time than I'd like to admit, I was pretty disgruntled, thinking God somehow favored Amy over me. Even worse, that she was a chosen "Isaac," and I was the rejected "Ishmael."

It was years later when I came to realize that the Isaac/Ishmael syndrome is not quite so easy to peg. The reason is ironically simple: God is after our heart attitudes, and our obedience and perseverance in whatever He has called us to do. His concern lies in the process of our personal growth, not simply in how far we have climbed the record label ladder. My career was just as important to Him as Amy's, but unfortunately it took many years of heartache and self-recrimination before I realized it.

Interestingly, some years later Amy and I met once again at a writer's meeting in Nashville. We shared the same publisher at the time. After the meeting, she came up to me and graciously said, "I know you from somewhere, but I can't place it." By then I had gotten free of the green-eyed monster, and we laughed at the memory together.

MY CREATIVE BACKGROUND

I have earned my way as a "creative" for over 30 years. During much of the 70s, I performed a one-woman show on the college circuit. I sang, spoke, played piano and guitar, wrote all my songs and material, designed my marketing materials, planned and orchestrated my tours, and recorded an album.

It was actually during this time in the mid-70s when I sensed God's call that I was to be a songwriter. I had written songs since the age of 13, but performing showed me that there was no greater thrill than to pour myself into a song and touch an audience with it. Embarking on my songwriting path, I invested all my energy into learning everything I could about the craft. I commuted to

Nashville; worked with renowned publishers; and with some of the top writers in the business, wrote all kinds of songs, everything from country to disco. I was relentless in my obedience to the call and in honing my songwriting expertise, but I was also forced into the practicality of helping us earn a living. My husband had begun graduate school, and I came off the road and started my first normal job as the first female disc jockey in Lexington, Kentucky. There I was also challenged to write and produce radio commercials. After a move to Denver, again I was challenged by the head of a recording studio to begin my first entrepreneurial venture: a jingle production company. During the 1978-79 recession, I segued into promotional work for Denver's CBS affiliate where I won an Alfie Award for the best 60-second TV spot featuring original music.

In the early 80s after our move to Georgia, I began my own advertising agency in order to support my songwriting pursuits. Creative Concepts Advertising initially began as a jingle writing/producing company, but mushroomed after I implemented a creative strategy God gave me in 1985 to help local businesses in Northeast Georgia. I later learned that God's larger plan for my business expansion was to enable me to survive as a single mother, since my husband would soon leave me.

This idea was actually the first of many creative business solutions given to me, not only for my personal survival, but also as a way to help others. The concept, which challenged existing FCC broadcast rulings at the time, took nine months to develop. I created an entirely new paradigm of broadcast production which I termed M.A.G.I.C. Spots (Multi-Advertiser Group Image Campaigns). Through them, small-town businesses could be grouped together in a single commercial and share the cost of a major-market advertising campaign. The success of these M.A.G.I.C. spots not only enabled these businesses to grow, but it grew my advertising agency into one of the most respected agencies in Northeast Georgia as well. Though my previous expertise was in jingles and broadcast commercials, I was forced to stretch creatively again as two of my initial three M.A.G.I.C. clients asked me to handle their advertising and promotional work. To do so, however, required that I learn a new set of creative skills—graphic design and layout. Soon, I became adept in designing logos, print ads, business proposals, brochures and direct mail campaigns, as well as placing media buys and managing entire promotional and image campaigns. In retrospect, I must say that the birth of a creative idea is one of the greatest adrenaline rushes in life. In a later chapter, I will discuss it further and suggest ways to become more open to these glimpses into divine illumination.

The 80s stretched me into yet another arena after Tom and I adopted our son, Tyler. Though I was ecstatic about my new role as a mother, my trips to Nashville ended as did my musical dreams, or so I thought.

One day a friend said, "I don't want to see you give up your music. Let me help you apply for a grant. What have you always wanted to do?"

Finally, I replied, "I've always wanted to write a musical," but reasoned I would write the music while someone else wrote the story. I was advised, however, that to increase my chances for a grant, I should write everything. So I said I would try. But what to write about? I waited for my next big idea, which finally came the night of auditions for a theatrical musical production where I was hired as music director. Never had I been involved in theater before, and never had I been a musical director. But I was hired to produce instrumental tracks on my newly purchased recording equipment for which I had no clue how to operate...yet!

A young African-American woman auditioned *a cappella,* but there were no parts for black actors. Why she was there I'll never know, but I will forever be grateful. Her voice blew me away. It was then that I knew I was to write a black musical, one that would showcase undiscovered talent like hers. The year was 1986, and there were no contemporary black musicals at that time. Weeks later, I received a letter from the governor bestowing the grant and informing me I had one year to write this musical. My only problem was that my husband had just declared he didn't want to be married anymore! Now as a single mother trying to write a black musical, I faced my greatest creative challenge at the worst personal time of my life.

My assignment, however, turned out to be a gift from God because it was a creative way to channel my hurt and anger. That year changed my life for until then, I had never written anything longer than a 3-minute song. During those 12 months, one passage in the Bible captured my thoughts: "In everything there is a season...there is a time to mourn and a time to dance" (Eccl. 3:1-4). Writing the musical I entitled *A Time To Dance* became an exercise in faith that God would one day bring me from my time of mourning to a time of dancing.

In 1987, I received a phone call from a producer who had read my fledgling script and wanted to discuss staging the musical. During our initial lunch meeting, David Thomas, artistic director of the ART Station Theater in Atlanta, said, "I'm sorry to stare at you, but I have read your script and listened to your music, and never knew until this moment that you were white." I smiled and replied, "David, you've given me the greatest compliment you could ever give me as a writer, for if these characters, songs, and the overall story rang true inside of you, then I succeeded as a writer."

A Time To Dance was produced first in 1989 and has since won 11 musical awards. Throughout the following pages, you will see how it was to change my life again eleven years later.

CHAPTER 2

The Origin of a *Creative*

The origin of creativity is found in the first chapter of Genesis, the fifth word, to be precise. "In the beginning (long before anything existed) God *created*..." The word "create" comes from the Hebrew word *bará* (pronounced baw-rah´) and is used 46 times in the Old Testament. It is used always with God as the subject and carries with it the meaning that God shaped, formed, fashioned, created from nothing, and called into being everything with a designated plan or purpose in mind. The concept of creation apart from the destiny for which it was created is foreign to the Scriptures. By the mere fact that something is created carries with it the understanding that it has a divine design or intended purpose. Sadly, so few of us truly understand, much less realize, our unique destinies and if there were only one motivation for writing this book, it would be to help you identify, clarify, and articulate your unique and wonderful destiny. (More on this topic is found in chapter five.)

THE FIRST CREATIVE

Notice that Genesis 1:1 reads, "In the beginning *God* created..." The act of creation is a divine one. It involves birthing something new that did not exist before, and the glory of that act is what separates God from every other supernatural being. The entire first chapter of Genesis is a litany of all that God created from nothing. The thought or seed concept of creation originated with Him...the how-to originated with Him...the intended purpose originated with Him. Not only did this gift find its source in Him, but it was limitless in its expression. God was not just adept at creating porcupines; He was the Creative Mastermind behind the entire animal kingdom! You see, it is the glory of God to bring to life that which was not. That is how He is most glorified. We tend to think that if someone is creative, his gifts are restricted to one or two areas. On the contrary, God is glorified most when our creative gifting is able to manifest itself in countless arenas. As we become more and more free to operate in our creative heritage, we glorify our Creator all the more, for His creative flow never ceases. Talk about creative problem-solving—no one is like our God! So what if His people were trapped between Pharoah's army and the Red Sea! He is the God who made a way through the sea for His people. During their wilderness wanderings, He showed forth His creative prowess time and time again: He brought forth water from a rock, manufactured manna out of thin air, blew quails in from all parts of the world and dropped them out of the sky, and caused springs to miraculously appear in the desert. He is the same God today and has endowed each one of us with that same creative ability.

With man, God truly did a different thing: He took dirt, molded it into a unique shape, breathed life into it, and said, "Let us make man in our image, after our likeness." That breath carried with it divine DNA and is our unique heritage as mankind. Possessing that divine attribute of creativity separates us from the animal kingdom. Yes, we can procreate like the animals and multiply ourselves, but only men and women have the ability to create something entirely new—to cause to come to life that which was not—and exercise dominion through it.

THE CREATIVE'S KEY ATTRIBUTES

To understand more fully our creative roles, we also need to understand two additional concepts. First is the concept of proprietorship or ownership. There is a maternal or paternal pride inherently birthed along with the process of creation; but more than mere pride, it's a deep emotional bonding that takes place between a creator and that which he/she creates.

Throughout Scripture, we see this attribute portrayed in God's unending love for His children, how He pursues them passionately, yearns for them to return to Him, and disciplines their wayward hearts to bring them home. God's heart is the steadfast love of a husband longing for his bride, a shepherd protecting his sheep, a mother tending to every need of her child. In like manner, the creator of a song, a book, a painting, or a piece of sculpture has that same sense of proprietorship inherently within him. Our creation is an extension of who we are. It contains our very essence, our "breath," which is why creatives notoriously have a difficult time handling criticism. Everything we *are* lies within our creation. That's a good thing. It belongs within us and is part of that divine DNA we were given. Sadly, many an inspired work has been derailed because we have failed to exercise appropriate proprietorship. Only recently have I come to understand and accept it as a part of who I am as a creative made in the image of God.

In 1990, I had a significant experience with God, wherein I sensed with every fiber of my being that I was to write a screenplay called *The Seventieth Week,* based on Daniel's prophecy concerning the last seven years of mankind, in preparation for the Lord's return. I was overwhelmed by both this experience, and this request. Quite frankly, I was shaking. Yes, I had written a musical, but I knew nothing about writing screenplays. With tears streaming down my face, I pleaded, "Lord, surely You have someone more experienced in Hollywood to do this. I don't know anybody there, or anything about doing what You're asking me to do!" The very next day, the devotional I happened to be reading was from Oswald Chambers' *My Utmost For His Highest.* The day's lesson was in Isaiah: "And I heard the voice of the Lord saying, 'Whom shall I send, and who will go for us?' Then I said, 'Here am I! Send me" (Isa. 6:8-9). These verses jumped off the page to me. God spoke to my heart, "I didn't say, 'Isaiah, I want you to do such and such.' I simply revealed My heart; Isaiah heard it and responded."

For the first time I began to understand that for that season of time in 1990 I was tapped into the heart of God. I heard what was on His heart: He wanted this screenplay written. His heart was bent on preparing the world and His people for what was to come. My responsibility was simply to respond. I had the same free will choice that Isaiah had. Would I do it? Would I heed God's request and follow through? That day, I told the Lord, "Yes, I will commit myself to do this." For the next seven years, I labored on this project. To do so required me to take time away from my ad agency and devote at least three hours a day to the task and to cut my income-earning potential in half. Not only did I have to research the biblical prophecies concerning the last days, but I also had to learn about global world affairs, the Middle East crisis, the New Age movement, and international financial systems as well as figure out how the entertainment industry operated. Once this screenplay was finished, how was I to pitch it? And to whom? How is pitching done in Hollywood? The questions and the challenges seemed endless.

Doors began to open for me in the entertainment industry. I began my second company, Quadra Entertainment, and through it began to pitch *The Seventieth Week*. It received considerable interest, but I was still very much an industry neophyte. More doors opened, however. I became President of Georgia's Women In Film and served several years on the board of Women in Film and Television International, as well as the Georgia Film, Video and Music Advisory Commission. You can imagine my disappointment watching other works surface and achieve a measure of success: *The Omega Code*, the *Left Behind* series...each work touching on the similar themes God had impressed on my heart to do. Frankly, I was disgruntled. After all, I started my project before these! I heard God first! I became angry with God. "Why did You ask me to do this if You were going to have someone else come along and do it first?" His answer? "You heard My heart. So did they. You were obedient to My call. So were they. I care more about your obedience and your perseverance than I care that you beat them to the punch." Ouch. The first of many such lessons understanding the farther-reaching purposes of God. It's all about the process, the journey, and personal obedience—not who becomes famous or prosperous.

The Seventieth Week sat on a shelf for several more years. From time to time I would ask the Lord about it, but I was involved in other projects. In fact, I had undergone a devastating financial loss following my inaugural venture as a theatrical producer, and I didn't ever want to pitch anything again. I was broken. My heart was gone and the creative juices stagnant. One day, an actress friend of mine admonished me saying, "You are the only one who can pick yourself up and start pitching your projects again." She was right. I had a choice—to sit there and grumble about the injustices of life or "show up to my creative call." What my friend's bluntness had done was to shock me out of my introspective paralysis. I could no longer stay in the ditch if I wanted to progress on my journey. How much we need the encouragement of our friends!

On January 6, 2003, to begin the new year with renewed commitment, I sat down in front of the computer and asked the Lord to give me the ideas of what He wanted me to do. Suddenly, the entire project illumined inside my mind. I saw it! It was *The Seventieth Week*, but in an entirely new configuration as a 10-part television documentary series. This way, I could utilize all the knowledge I had gained over the last decade plus include everything I had learned the past two years, a key to beginning this series. By morphing it into a non-fictional documentary series, production time would be much faster and more immediate than a film, and I would be able to adapt to current world changes. In that one 24-hour period, everything since 1990 made sense. I connected with two producer friends of mine whose job it was to pitch the project to Hollywood and pull in the other people we needed to round out the key players. That was when I began to learn the unforgettable lesson of the meaning of proprietorship.

One of my producing partners called one day and asked if I would mind sharing the "Created By" credit for the series, explaining that it was easier to do business in Hollywood if one possesses that particular credit. I got off the phone as quickly as I could. "YES, I DO MIND!" was my thought. The more I thought about it, the madder I got. I minded very much! I paced all over my office, and wrestled with guilt and self-condemnation. Am I so selfish I can't share a title? Am I so control-oriented that I have to be the "big cheese"? I hated myself for these emotions, so much so that I was afraid to bring them before the Lord for His scrutiny. I was afraid to hear Him say, "You are horrible, selfish, and a control-freak!" I finally became so miserable that I decided to do nothing, until God gave me clarity. Even if it was to clarify my unworthiness as a creative.

The next day I was spending my regular time with the Lord and happened to be reading Isaiah 5 that describes the great care with which God cared for His people. God depicts Israel as a vineyard, and poetically expresses how He personally, meticulously planted the choicest vines, removed the rocks, built a watchtower, and prepared for a glorious harvest. What happened, however, was that Israel refused to honor their Creator, went their own way, and grew up as a wild grapevine. What did God do? He was so jealous over His creation that He destroyed it rather than have it produce that which He did not intend.

The passage spoke powerfully to the zeal with which a creator should protect his creation. God spoke to my heart and I was shown a powerful lesson: my zealous protectionism over my project was a vital part of the creator's role, not a character flaw. It wasn't selfishness; rather, it was a stewardship responsibility that needed to be embraced. You see, there is an important shepherding aspect that goes along with creative gifting, and the one to whom the idea is given is also entrusted with the responsibility to be its shepherd. Why? Because only that person carries within him the strongest emotional bond for its care and survival. This protectionism applies not only to a television series, but to an invention, a new business venture, or a child. The two qualities (the creating and the shepherding) go hand in hand and are both critical to the proper growth and development of what is being created.

It never ceases to amaze me that the Word of God is truly a "lamp to our feet and a light to our path." In one split second I was freed from the feelings of guilt and self-condemnation. I was also enlightened to understand the difference between a creator's role and a producer's. It helped me see why so many inspired projects crumble. You see, creatives in general tend to be on the ethereal (some call it flaky), non-follow-through side of the cerebral cortex. Thus it is very tempting for us to hand our creation over to someone else to shepherd—someone who is not as emotionally bonded to the work. Think about it: we don't give our children to someone else to raise, so why should we expect others to raise our creative children? One of the goals of the Creativity Training Institute that I have established is to teach creatives to learn to shepherd their own projects and birth them into their destinies.

SEEING THE END RESULT

The second attribute connected with being a creator is that a true creator is given the ability to "see" the end result. I will discuss this in more detail in Chapter 5, but suffice it to say that a true creator of something is given an internal "vision" of what that thing is meant to become. I have a dear friend who is a gifted sculptor. One day she showed me the marble stone she had just bought. With the excitement of a child, she couldn't wait to start work on it. I stared at the stone and saw nothing. To me, it was just a rock. But she saw something inside of it. It spoke to her! She had learned over the years to hear the voice of the stone when it spoke and to act on it. There is tremendous power released when we embrace this creative quality and act on it. Several weeks later I went over for dinner, and there in her foyer was the most exquisite sculpture. Like a proud mother, she grinned from ear to ear as I effused, "I can't believe you brought this out of a stone! You are a genius; it's beautiful!"

Lest you think that this creative envisioning attribute is only for those we normally think of as "artists," my late husband Mike was creatively gifted when it came to numbers. It never ceased to amaze me that numbers spoke to him in the same way the stone spoke to my friend and in the same way that ideas speak to me. That speaking is the beckoning call of the creative gifting.

The following chapters describe how we can hear the voice of creativity and act upon it.

CHAPTER 3

What's Your CQ?

The initials CQ stands for "Creativity Quotient." Genesis clearly teaches that we are each given an innate ability to create, for creativity is part of the divine DNA that is our inheritance. The questions naturally arise: "Why do some people seem to have more than others?" or "How can we know how much we have?"

A key spiritual principle is found in Jesus' parable of the talents in Matthew 25. The story begins in verse 14 when at the beginning of a journey, the master entrusts a certain amount of his property (i.e., talents) to three servants: "To one he gave five talents, to another two, to another one, to each according to his ability." The word "talent" referred to a monetary unit. In New Testament times, the talent was not a weight of silver as it was in Old Testament times. Rather, the Roman-Attic talent comprised 6,000 denarii or drachmas, equal to about $375. The master then went away, and upon his return, called his servants to give account for how they had each fared in their stewardship. The ones who were given five talents and two talents, respectively, both doubled their money, whereas the third one buried his one talent out of fear of losing it altogether and lost out completely. The master took it away, calling him "slothful," and gave it to the one who had earned ten talents. Jesus poignantly said, "To every one who has, will more be given, and he will have abundance; but from him who has not, even what he has will be taken away" (Matt. 25:29).

We can draw application for our creative giftings in that as we are faithful to use and move freely in the amount of creativity God has given us, more will be given. The converse is also true: if we do not use wisely the amount we've been given, it can be taken away and given to someone else. Remember, God gives "to each according to his ability." He knows exactly how much or little we can manage.

I often chastised myself for not spending time perfecting any one gift. Thus, I lived in defeat, thinking I was disappointing God. I reasoned, "If only I had concentrated on *one* thing, like playing the piano, perhaps I could have really excelled, and thus glorified God more in that ability." I am learning now, however, that my gifting seems to be the free-flow of creativity operating within many arenas, and that perhaps He gave me this one so that I could relate to so many different kinds of creatives.

DISTINGUISHING MARKS

There are people who are wonderfully creative in their particular field—creative business people, accountants, teachers, politicians, doctors, visionary entrepreneurs—professionals who express creativity in their particular line of work. There seems to be a distinction, however, between creative people in general and the "creative" as we have been discussing, who are uniquely wired for creativity. These individuals share certain traits in common.

Creatives have a never-ending flow of ideas. Many times these ideas carry with them the sense of brilliance. We know deep down, of course, that these ideas come from a Source much greater than ourselves, which then infuse us with a sense of awe of the greatness and power of our Creator, and a feeling of responsibility for following through with the ideas given. I remember one day a few years ago, I was relaxing by the swimming pool, reading a business magazine, which has always proved good fodder for ideas. Suddenly an idea came into my mind. Over the years I have learned to tell if an idea is *just* an idea, or *really* an idea. This experience was the latter. Throughout the afternoon, the idea cascaded into my mind in many layers. It was a thrilling moment: I was birthing an "idea with legs"—always the best kind. In other words, it didn't just have one application. It had many and could benefit a lot of people. I couldn't wait to get to my legal pad and begin to flesh it out in words. It was a big one and took months of thought, prayer, and counseling with my business coach before I could determine what I needed to do about it. Who was it intended for? For me or my chapter of Women in Film/Atlanta, of which I was then president? Was it something I needed to act on now or in the future? I like to compare the idea-birthing experience to a surfer waiting for the big wave. When you experience one, you endure the long wait for the next one because you know it's going to be one heckuva ride! This "gift" or ability is one that can be developed over time, and this book will touch on ways to cultivate the flow of ideas. The downside of this gift, however, is that often so many ideas come that we don't know which ones to follow through with, which can lead to artistic paralysis.

Creatives hear and sense things others do not. The majority of people live in a world of noise. Many cannot function without a TV or radio. As an introverted NF (Intuitive Feeler), and perhaps because I am a composer, I function best in quiet, for it is here that I hear the ideas, the melodies, the lyrics. It is the world to which I am accustomed, and thankfully, there is no set rule here. If you function best in audio-chaos, that doesn't mean you are not creative. We have to learn our own way, and understand how we best hear the inner voice. Over the years, I have learned to develop my intuitive instincts, and I guard them as if protecting gold or silver. My coach, Mariette Edwards, once told me: "Your ideas are your wealth." She's right. The great success philosopher, Napoleon Hill recounted the times he made fortunes and lost them. He concluded in his later years that one's true wealth lies not in the wealth itself but in the God-given ability to create the ideas that lead to wealth. Recessions and depressions come and go, partnerships go sour, you get fired or lose your top client, but no one can take away your "vein of gold," as Julia Cameron discusses in one of her sequels to her classic book, *The Artist's Way*.

Creatives need to devote disciplined time to their craft. To learn a new creative discipline (such as songwriting, poetry, screenwriting, writing book proposals, graphic design, etc.), there is always a large amount of time devoted to the discipline itself. In other words, what are the rules of the trade? A creative has to master the "form" before the content has the freedom to "flow." I had been studying the screenwriting craft for several years, which involved trips to L.A. to study with the "masters," so to speak. My library is filled with the top "how-to" books on everything from plot structuring to character delineation, the proper use of mythology, humorous dialogue, and on and on. I've read every one. The mind becomes so consumed with the "rules" that for a season of time, the feelings are buried in the form.

As with all creative categories in my life, I have actual files wherein I store my ideas. I learned early on that if all the ideas that came to me floated around in my head 24 hours a day, I would need a lobotomy. Therefore, whenever a good idea comes, I file it in the appropriate Ideas File: songs, musicals, films, books, magazine articles, dialogue, television series, and business ideas.

Creatives need to develop their intuitive sense to make their way through the creative journey. In March 2001, I began one of my toughest creative challenges in mounting my first production, not as the writer only, but now as executive producer: raising money for the world premiere of my re-staged musical *A Time To Dance*. Naturally, I sought advice from successful businessmen who had experience in raising venture capital. Their advice was two-pronged: 1) Don't waste your seed money having a function at the country club to present your business plan because no one will come; and 2) Don't bother presenting the investment opportunity to women because they don't know how to read a prospectus and would just go home and show it to their husbands.

The more I thought about their advice, the more it didn't sit right. Everything in me screamed to do just the opposite. I decided to have a luncheon at the country club targeting exclusively women. Over 80 came and a third of them indicated an interest in being part of my investment team. From that one luncheon I was asked to speak to five women's investment groups in the area. I ended up raising the amount I was seeking, and out of 115 individuals that comprised my investment team, 106 were women. It pays to listen to your inner voice.

Creatives often have a sense of personal destiny. Whereas other personality types may long for freedom, or power, or to be needed by and useful to their organizational unit, the creative's plumb line is his need to have meaning and purpose in life. He feels he was put on earth for a particular purpose and spends his life looking for it. It is here that many get derailed. We fall easily into the thinking pattern that we've missed it or that we're not doing what we should be doing, which in turn creates a restlessness to move on to the next thing, often ending jobs or relationships mid-course. This restlessness can lead to depression, where we think we've failed in what we were born to do. Once we hit depression, our internal light goes out and death is but a shovel away.

Often creatives' ideas are prophetic, or ahead of their time. How frustrating it is when something in popular culture becomes a big trend, and we realize it was something we created or wrote years ago, when the trend was something else! When I first wrote my musical, it was the mid-80s. There were no contemporary black musicals at the time, and the market was not open to inspirational, family-oriented entertainment. How times have changed. Fast forward 15 years, and inspirational black musicals are now big business!

When I finished writing my "revenge-comedy" *Retribution*, I took it out to my then literary agent in Hollywood. The first words out of his mouth were, "No studio will look at it. Women over 45 don't go to movies. There's no market it for it whatsover!" I looked at him with total amazement, thinking to myself, *That cannot be true. Why would I have spent a year and a half of my life working on this movie?* Everything in me knew he was wrong, but who was I—a neophyte with no track record. The year was 1996. Shortly after he turned me down, *The First Wives Club* premiered to box office records! It had first been a bestselling book, which I had purposely *not* read because I didn't want to subconsciously assimilate anyone else's ideas. The only thing I knew was that the book dealt with revenge by women who had been dumped. A similar theme, only my film went in its own very personal direction. Goldie Hawn,

Bette Midler, and Diane Keaton were soon plastered on magazine covers everywhere. I tore one out and faxed it to my agent, with a short note: "There IS a market for films targeting 45+ year old women. There just isn't anything out there that we care to see!" Personally, internally, I was validated. My instincts were right on, only my timing, once again, was off!

Creatives often have "tent-making" professions to help us survive while we are doing our art. My work in advertising has been my bread and butter since the late 70s. It remains an excellent parallel field because it keeps me on the cutting edge of communicating to the masses. In 1994, when I began Quadra Entertainment, the plan was to develop two future income streams so that when I reach retirement age, I would have my writing career to provide another source of income. I may be too old to write commercials at age 70 or 75, but hopefully, the wisdom and insights gained over a lifetime will enrich my stories and my characters and serve to inspire audiences.

This plan was challenged several years ago when I was presented with an opportunity to merge with a larger ad agency. It was a tempting offer, to have an equity stake in a sure thing with professionals I respect. But the closer I got into "due diligence," the more uneasy I became. I realized that when the inspiration hit to write a book, or a screenplay, or a musical, I would not be able to do it, for I would have made an overriding commitment to the agency. Ultimately, I turned down the offer and continue to this day on my own creative journey.

Creatives feel things deeper than most people. I never really understood this principle until I went through my divorce. I've always considered myself fairly level-headed and business-minded, and am perceived by others as very "together." During the divorce, however, my emotions were on a roller coaster. I had never experienced such a degree of rage, hurt, and betrayal. My precious neighbor, Marilyn Williamson, would patiently listen to all my tirades and horror stories. Marilyn is one of these practical, no-nonsense, to-the-point people I have come to greatly value in my life. I remember one such outpouring of grief and she calmly remarked, "I've decided that you feel things deeper than most people." I was taken back. What? You mean everybody doesn't feel things like this? It was a new revelation to me.

Since then, I've come to view my times of personal crisis in a new light. It's as if the camera re-focuses on the same scene and a new dimensional layer emerges. Several years ago I was going through a difficult emotional trial. Many hurts and fears from the past were rearing their ugly heads, and I felt like an abandoned, lonely child. In the midst of my self-shaming, the focus shifted and that inner voice said, "If you are going through this, imagine how many others are as well. Use it. Write it." In a split-second, the whole incident now served a grander, nobler purpose—anointing my writing with a story and characters that not only touched me deeply (because I was living it), but went on to touch everyone who has read it.

As a writer, I began to see my creative life as a calling, and one of the things I was called on to do was go through difficult times in order to encourage others who were to take a similar journey.

Creatives have the ability to mirror the heart and soul of our culture. The majority of people get up, go to work, come home, and find enjoyment in their family, friends, and recreational activities. Nothing wrong with that, unless you are a creative. We have an innate ability to be the reflective soul of our society, the one who mirrors its ills and its genius. Our gifts can be used to uplift and inspire, or they can be used to denigrate and destroy wholesome morals and values. Same gift...channeled in two directions.

We've all seen this gift in operation. I'll never forget the horror of seeing Sir Anthony Hopkins' portrayal of Hannibal Lecter. Through his acting talent, he mirrored the soul of a serial killer. He didn't just play the part of Lecter; he became the man. There is a huge difference between actors who are skilled in a technique and those like Hopkins who have this mirroring gift.

I served on the board of Women in Film and Television

International and attended our Summit in London in October 2000. Paul Howarth, the British Council Director of Film, addressed our delegates and said, "I believe you, as women, have a particularly important role to play in bringing a sense of moral responsibility to the entertainment industry." Irish filmmaker, Mary Raftery, then told of the months she spent uncovering a generation of children ripped apart from their families and brought up in church-run institutions. Her chilling documentary, *States of Fear,* exposed the horrifying sexual abuse these children suffered, and her film resulted in bringing the entire nation to its knees.

Creatives are vulnerable to derailment. I cannot prove empirically what I am about to say. Rather, this belief comes from years of observation and a visceral intuitive sense. I believe that creatives are uniquely vulnerable to derailment because we threaten to glorify God and resolve the many problems of the world. Derailment by whom? Remember, the creative act is reserved only for the One True God. Additionally, the Scriptures refer to opposing forces in the spiritual realm who resort to any number of tactics in an attempt to destroy the divine DNA (i.e., creativity) within God's people. Where there is good, there is also evil. We do not function in a vacuum, and because creatives are uniquely sensitive to the spirit arena, we are particularly vulnerable to this battleground.

One such tactic of the evil side is to mimic the creative voice of God and lure the creative into thinking it is God telling him to do something. How many films glorify violence, gross immorality, or predatory violence toward women or people of other races? Would our loving Father have called those films into being?

A second tactic is to target creatives for an unseen mental onslaught, to trap us in self-defeat, unrealized dreams, financial despair, and spiritual derailment. My heart breaks over so many gifted people who lie wounded in the desert. I recognize them because I, too, have triggered more than one land mine of my own, and lay maimed in many a wilderness. To my fellow creatives: please hear me when I say that you have not failed. Rather, you are being opposed by an unseen enemy who is very threatened by your creative gifting and who would love nothing better than to see you give up and die.

For years my late husband Mike dreamed of starting his own homebuilding company. His mind was flooded with creative ideas: the type homes he would build and how he would organize and run the company. This venture held within it a deep spiritual connection for him because he was certain God was calling him to do it and giving him the ideas he needed every step of the way. The time came for him to step forth in faith and leave his present job to start this venture. We were both exhilarated. He chose a businessman as his partner whose job it was to put up the capital; Mike was to be general manager. The partner, however, in order to raise more money, sold Mike's shares out from under him. Suddenly his four-year-old dream disintegrated before his eyes. In an attempt to save the customers who were building their dream homes and protect the company's cash flow, he had no choice but to leave his own company, the one that he birthed. It couldn't support the two of them, and the partner was holding all the cards (i.e., the money). The experience broke his heart, and he never ventured forth like that again.

I'll never forget a conversation we had shortly before his death. He was remarking how alive I had become and how I had changed. This was during a time when I had been intensely working through some of my issues and freeing the creative spirit within me. I said to him, "Honey, you still have that little boy in you who dreams and wants to do and create things." I'll never forget his sobering reply: "I want that little boy dead." He died two months later. Who else but the enemy of our souls would want to quash the creative energy God gave him and leave him with no vision? "Where there is no vision, the people perish" (Prov. 11:14).

A third oft-seen tactic is when creatives are lured away from glorifying God with their gifts. These gifts are given freely by our Creator before the foundation of the world. "For the gifts and the call of God are irrevocable" (Rom. 11:29). That means He does not take them away if we don't use them wisely. How we choose to use them is all part of our free will. It is a choice to use them for good, or use them for evil. I need to say here that I don't believe that God is pleased only when we use our gifts in the church or synagogue. That would go against everything God commissioned us to do in Genesis—to exercise dominion as godly men and women in every aspect of our society. Rather, it's the inner motives of gift usage that the opposing forces try to skew.

Because I am in the entertainment business, I rub shoulders with brilliantly creative people. Many are doing ennobling work with their gifts: acting, directing, producing inspiring films and television shows. Sadly, however, many are lured into lowering their gifts in the pursuit of money, fame, or self-glory.

Chapter 10 is entirely devoted to uncovering the most common ways that creative people are targeted for derailment. By recognizing our personal mine fields, we learn to avoid being tripped up by them. More importantly, we become stronger in our resolve to fulfill the creative destiny God has for each one of us.

Creatives are particularly wired to tap into the spiritual realm. I know creatives from all parts of the entertainment industry, and by and large, every one of them is deeply spiritual. I don't think we can function as creatives without the realization that our ideas and abilities come from a Higher Source. We are humbled by it. The difference lies perhaps in the creative's understanding of who or what that Source is. I have friends who regularly consult psychics to align them with their path. Others consult Tarot cards. Others meditate and burn incense. Still others write of an impersonal Higher Intelligence.

Over 30 years ago I made a decision to follow the Lord and study His Word, the Scriptures. As far as learning the creative journey, I made a commitment to test every new wave of modern theory to see if there were a scriptural basis, for therein I would have confidence I was on solid ground. Unfortunately the Bible doesn't have a chapter called "Creativity Training." The principles are gleaned over time, searched out as if searching for hidden treasure.

Cry out for insight, raise your voice for understanding; if you seek it like silver and search for it as for hidden trea-

sures, then you will understand the fear of the Lord and find the knowledge of God (Prov. 2:3-5).

It is my belief that only our Creator can truly instruct us in how to create, and more importantly, how to find meaning in our creativity. We are made in His image, and He has communicated everything we need to know about the creative journey. But His truths are not for everyone. They are given only to those to seek, who listen, and who are motivated to hear the truth.

I was motivated because I was miserable. My heart had been broken, my dreams shattered, and my creative longings unfulfilled. Time and time again I would reach a particular place in my creative journey—so close—only to watch the whole thing unravel. Where was I going wrong? Was I sabotaging myself? Was I not worthy? Was I reaping the effects of some unconfessed sin? Something within me knew I was being blocked, but I had no clue what it was, much less what to do about it. I couldn't stand one more day with this nagging feeling that I wasn't doing what I was supposed to be doing. I had to know.

Since early 1998, I became relentless in my search. I studied books by noted success gurus, went through therapy, hired a business coach, attended a creative support group where we worked through our issues, and at the same time faithfully studied the Scriptures and journaled my findings. This book is the culmination of that search. What I learned changed my creative life. It enabled me to break with my old patterns of stalled starts. It gave me the inner fuel to destroy former self-limitations. As the old spiritual says, "I saw the light!"

Once I saw it and began to apply it, my life went from reverse to fast forward. In 14 months, I put up the seed money, hired an attorney and formed a new venture, developed a business plan and financial projections, raised money from investors, negotiated contracts with my creative team, hired the large cast and crew and mounted the World Premiere of my re-staged musical *A Time To Dance*. People who had known me for years couldn't believe that this same shy, insecure writer somehow blossomed into a theatrical producer. I was transformed from a dreamer to a doer.

CHAPTER 4

Identify Your
Personal *Genetic Code*

I have a good friend who was a Hollywood star in years past. Though extremely gifted and experienced in many areas, she tearfully expressed one day, "I feel so lost...like I've missed my chance at doing something significant." Her problem surfaced when she watched other people's successes and decided, "Oh, I could do that." or "I have done that before." Yes, she could, and she did. But should she now? That's where the core issue lies, that all-too-common creative paralysis that she is working to address.

Just what is this angst? It is that question mark emblazoned inside our hearts. If we try to put it into words, it goes something like this: "Who am I...really?" We go through life having succeeded at some things, failed at others, and at some point in life—often a personal catastrophe divinely given to get our attention—we come to a painful time of real soul-searching. I have had several such times in my life. There's no getting around it; they are excruciating. And yet, after coming through them, there is an unbelievable sense of freedom and self-awareness that I wouldn't trade for anything in the world.

In preparing for this book, I took an informal poll among several groups of creative people. On the questionnaire I wrote down a series of topics and asked them to rank their degree of interest from one to ten, ten being the highest interest. Two of the topics that ranked the highest were: "How can you discover your unique gifts?" and "You sense you are 'called' to a creative work, but how do you find what it is you are called to do?" These findings were enlightening in that they underscored the fact that all of us have a need to understand and connect with our individual destinies.

Understanding comes with enlightenment from our Creator's perspective. After all, He created us. But for what did He create us?

Close your eyes and imagine a pumpkin seed. The secret to our destiny lies with this seed. A pumpkin seed is destined to become a healthy, full-grown pumpkin. Could it ever become anything else? No. Why not? Even though its seed may look like a zucchini seed, it will nonetheless end up a pumpkin because it was genetically coded to do so by the Creator.

The word "destiny" is defined by Webster as, "Something to which a person is decreed, assigned, or set apart to do beforehand." This definition is certainly in alignment with the Genesis account, for this pumpkin seed was destined "beforehand," at the very beginning of time, to be a pumpkin. In like manner, your life is a seed that is also genetically coded. It holds promise and a sense of destiny as to what it is designed to be. You were specifically made for a unique purpose and are of far more value to God than a pumpkin. The psalmist says, "Your eyes beheld my unformed substance; in your book were written, every one of them, the days that were formed for me" (Psalm 139:16). God was there at the beginning of your conception, and will be there when your earthly life is finished. In between are appointed days that we have on this earth, days that he has numbered for each one of us. How are we spending those days? What were we destined to become? Are we doing it? Are we certain? Our heavenly Father does not want us to go through life feeling empty, misdirected, or growing wild in some foreign soil serving very little purpose. He wants us to know the wonder and magnificence that lies within the seeds that are our lives.

WHO ARE YOU?

Before we go deeper into self-discovery, I need to ask: Have you ever asked God what He made you to be? The psalmist says, "Know that the Lord is God; It is he that made us, and not we ourselves. We are his people, and the sheep of his pasture" (Psalms 100:3). There is a close relationship between a shepherd and his sheep. He knows each one intimately, and they know him. God is telling us He is our Shepherd, not some impersonal Source. He made us, so it follows that He knows exactly what He made us to do and to be. He delights in revealing His will, but we have to ask Him.

In the 70s and 80s, the "in" thing was to be a generalist. Take songwriting, for instance. During that time, to be a good songwriter required that you be proficient at both melodies and lyrics, able to play guitar and keyboard. It also helped if you could sing and demo your songs on your own studio equipment, which of course you had to learn to use. That was the portrait of a real songwriter.

I'll never forget the pride I felt when I learned how to program the drum synthesizer by myself. Finally, I thought, *I won't need anyone else to demo my songs. I can do everything!* Wrong. It didn't take long for me to realize that I didn't enjoy experimenting with drum sounds, studying which part of the stereo spectrum the "high hat" should be. Who cares? Somebody does, but it wasn't me. Thus, I began to learn that in the realm of original music, my passion was in the creation of the song itself: the hook, the lyrics, the chord progression, the structure, the melody, and the emotional impact it would have on a listener.

The music I wrote for *A Time To Dance* has received rave reviews. The Atlanta Journal-Constitution wrote, "The music soars in *A Time To Dance*. Long's compositions are the heart and soul of the musical." I have no doubt, though, that I share that review with many others. Yes, I did write the songs. But Anthony Lockett produced the instrumental arrangements, Leslie Riley conceived the vocal arrangements, and singing sensations like Francine Reed communicated the songs with the magic that touched audiences. Each one of them are creatives in their own right.

THE LAW OF FOCUS

The irony of creative gifts is that, when properly used, they often spill over into other areas. Barbra Streisand is a perfect example. As a singer, she is unparalleled. As an actress, outstanding. Her creative talents have led her to take up directing and producing. There seems to be no limit to her creativity. Yet as a youth, if you were to say, "I want to be like Barbra Streisand," you'd get a cynical chuckle and a closed door. Why? Because people would assume that you don't know what you want to be when you grow up.

Everything in us fights against narrowing our focus. I recall one day sitting in the office of a powerful producer in Nashville. He listened to some of my songs, leaned over his desk and asked, "So, what do you really want to be? A writer or a singer?" I was dumbfounded. I thought to myself, "Why can't I be both?"

I was not able to answer the producer at that time, and my career stalled because of it. Yet it was an important crossroads. Some months later, I concluded that I was a writer. How? I reasoned that I sang well enough, but knew I wasn't any Streisand or Trisha Yearwood. Having sung jingles for years, I had learned to mimic whatever style I wanted to sing or whatever fit the song I'd just written. If you were to hear me sing songs from my musical, and if you closed your eyes, you would swear I am black. That is an ability all its own, but it prevented me from developing a unique vocal style. Understanding myself vocally, however, did eventually help me narrow my focus even further.

As a marketing professional, I understand the principles of marketing well. Companies who abide by the principles in the marketing classic *The 22 Immutable Laws of Marketing* succeed, and those who don't, fail. It's that simple, because there are laws or principles for marketing. These laws have to do with niching a company's brand in the mind of the audience. A company has to *know* what it wants to do, what widget it wants to make, what service it wants to offer, and how that widget or service is different from other companies in the market.

One of my favorite success stories is that of Federal Express. They were not the first delivery service to enter the marketplace. In fact, Emery Air Freight was the leader in air freight services: small packages, large packages, overnight, and delayed services. Anything you wanted to ship, you could ship with Emery. But Federal Express entered the market and shocked corporate America by becoming number one. How? By following the Law of Focus.

Had Federal Express adopted a marketing strategy that said,

"We are a delivery company just like Emery: We deliver anything: domestic, overseas, packages, you name it, only we're going to be better than Emery," they would have joined the corporate junkyard with the likes of Studebaker, MITS Altair 880 Computers, and New Coke. Instead, they narrowed their focus. You remember their original slogan: "When it absolutely, positively has to be there overnight." They focused *only* on overnight delivery, and now their name has become synonymous with the service it renders. Executives say, "Just fedex it to me." That's the mark of a leader. Because they started narrow (as did Streisand as a singer), they could expand categories (as they are doing now internationally) once they were accepted in the marketplace.[2]

BUILT-IN SENSE OF DESTINY

My coach says, "There is something inside you that knows what you are meant to do." She's right. There is. But often, it takes years to sift through our experiences and make sense of it all. Look at Moses—it took him 40 years to "name his seed."

The story of Moses, recounted in the book of Exodus, is a wonderful story that underscores that indeed we are called to do certain things, gifted for specific tasks by our Creator, and He patiently works with us throughout our lives until we finally "get the picture."

Moses was born an Israelite in Egypt, at the time Pharaoh passed an edict ordering all male Jewish babies to be killed. You remember the story: Pharaoh's daughter rescued Moses from the bulrushes, from certain death, and raised him as her own son. Moses was schooled and trained in all the wisdom of the Egyptians and was "mighty in his words and deeds" according to the account. When he was 40 years old, something in his heart led him to visit his people, the Israelites, and he had great compassion on them. In fact, he became so consumed with compassion that when one of his people was being abused by an Egyptian, Moses struck the Egyptian and killed him.

The apostle Paul recounts the story: "Moses supposed that his brethren understood that God was giving them deliverance by his

hand, but they did not understand." Not only did they not understand, they turned against Moses saying, "Who made you a ruler
and a judge over us? Do you want to kill me as you killed the
Egyptian yesterday?" (Acts 7:28)

The principle is very keen here: Moses had a "call" on his life.
There was something strongly fixed in his heart to save his people
and deliver them. But when he started to do it, he was soundly rejected. He failed and ran away to Midian where he hid for 40 years.
Now Midian is about as far in the middle of nowhere as he could go.
There Moses lived an obscure life, tending Jethro's sheep. He was so
burned by the rejection that he never ventured forth again, until
one day he saw a bush burning all by itself, that wasn't being consumed. Curious, he walked toward the bush to find out what was
going on. That's when the voice of the Lord called to him, "Moses,
put off your shoes from your feet, for the place on which you are
standing is holy ground" (Exod. 3:5). There in the wilderness, God
appeared to Moses and called him to do what he had been prepared
for his whole life: "free my people."

This story is pregnant with application:

God puts within us a sense of destiny. There was indeed something inside Moses that knew what he was to do. His instincts 40
years earlier were right on target. So what happened? Moses wasn't
yet ready, and the timing wasn't right for the Israelites to receive
Moses as their deliverer. It took 40 more years of slavery for them
to get so desperate as to truly cry out to God. Moses, however, took
their rejection personally and assumed his place was out in the
wilderness. The wilderness, however, was not his destiny.

God has His own timetable, not ours. Before Moses' calling
could be realized, he needed two things: 1) humility and 2) the
people's receptivity. It took 40 years for both to come to fruition.

At the time of his first "call," Moses was in the prime of his in-
tellectual and physical strength. By the time he received his second
call at the burning bush, he was just an 80-year-old shepherd,
having carved out a half-life in the wilderness. God knew all along

where he was, and that Moses was still His man for the job. At that bush, Moses was finally able to learn what many of us have had to: that when God calls us to do great things, we will succeed only when we are *forced to depend on His strength rather than our own.*

There may be some of you reading this who know beyond a shadow of a doubt what you've been called to do, yet you haven't done it yet. Henry and Richard Blackaby in *Experiencing God*, wrote,

> It is never a minor thing to know God's will and not do it. God calls this sin. We rationalize, we procrastinate; yet, in God's eyes, rationalization and procrastination are nothing more than disobedience. When we encounter God and He gives us a direction, it is not enough to write down the date in our journal, or even tell our friends. God's call is to obey.[3]

Freedom from creative bondage only comes through desperation. The period of bondage and slavery that the Israelites experienced was key to their being set free. They were enslaved by a cruel Pharaoh who forced them into slave labor for more than 400 years. From God's covenant with Abraham, they knew their destiny wasn't the slave labor camps of Egypt, but it took that long for them to truly cry out in repentance to God. Ultimately, they were delivered from bondage to their destiny and eventually given their promised land.

This story is central to understanding the journey for the creative. Before we receive clarity about what we are created to be and to do, we often experience bondage. We have a sense that we are trapped in a life that wasn't meant to be ours. Often that bondage is of our own making, like marrying the wrong person or feeling trapped in a non-blending family. I need to say here that if you find yourself in this type bondage, God would certainly not want you to break free of your responsibilities to your family. But He does want you to cry out to Him and let Him shed light on the journey for you despite your circumstances. Remember, He is the God who brings forth springs out of a desert, and water from a rock. He can bring ultimate good out of everything.

Be prepared to re-visit failure. Moses was called the second time to do the same thing he felt called to do the first time: free God's people. On the journey to claim our personal destiny, we often may have to re-visit an area wherein we experienced failure.

This principle hit home when I was faced with mounting the musical. From my human perspective, music had been taken out of my life. The door had been shut long ago, and I had failed. After the initial production of *A Time To Dance* in 1989, I tried desperately to market it because everything in me told me there was a need for an inspirational, family-oriented, contemporary black musical. Doors continued to close. I was white. Who was I to write a black musical? Rather than reason that the timing was just off, I concluded (like so many do) that I must have missed the call, that God didn't want me in music, and I had failed in my understanding of what He wanted me to do. I felt unworthy, somehow, and very depressed.

I turned my attention to screenwriting, concluding that perhaps my Creator started me out in music only to really get my attention at longer form writing. You can imagine my shock to hear the call a second time to do this musical—the very thing that had produced such feelings of personal failure years before.

The certainty of the call is always backed up with signs. Whatever you are called to do—if you know in your heart you are called by your Creator to do it—then you can be assured He will be with you to give you the ability and strength to carry it out. But therein lies the crux of the matter. Unless you have that complete certainty in what you are to do, you cannot exercise proper faith to ensure its successful completion. The Creator, however, wants us to know His design for us, and longs to communicate to us and to confirm it in many ways.

Moses was a stuttering, bumbling, scraggly shepherd when he got his call. And when he kept making excuses as to why he couldn't carry out the task, God patiently told him He would give him signs along the way. He told him exactly what to do at precisely the time he needed to know. Moses didn't conjure up his rod to turn into a snake; God told him that would be one of his signs.

In my journey with the musical, there were many signs and confirmations along my way as well. I remember when I was making individual pitches to potential investors. It was tough. To me, asking for money is the next worse thing to having a colonoscopy. Sure, I had done the homework: I had the projections and had created the business plan. But I had to call on people (often cold calls) and make my pitch. As a sensitive introvert, who hates all forms of rejection, I experienced one day that was particularly tough. There was a man who had been referred to me, but every time I tried to reach him by phone, he was always busy. I was told, "Go see the man. Just wait in his office until he sees you." I prayed, "Lord, I don't want to go. I'm terrified of rejection. But I believe You want me to do this, so I'm looking to You for a sign to show me I'm on the right path."

I waited in his office for an eternity and was finally ushered in. As I began my presentation, suddenly his eyes lit up. He said, "I am so excited to have this investment opportunity! Give me a few days to round up some of my friends. I believe they will want to hear about it too." I floated out of his office, thankful for the sign of encouragement God gave me, one of many He sustained me with during the grueling months of fundraising.

MOSES TURNS TO A CREATIVE

One of my favorite characters in the Bible is Bezalel, who is only mentioned a few times; nonetheless, he had a very unique calling. In Exodus, we read,

The Lord said to Moses, "See, I have called by name Bezalel the son of Uri, son of Hur, of the tribe of Judah: and I have filled him with the Spirit of God, with ability and intelligence, with knowledge and all craftsmanship, to devise artistic designs, to work in gold, silver, and bronze, in cutting stones for setting, and in carving wood, for work in every craft" (Exod. 31:1-5).

Talk about a creative! Bezalel had the God-given knowledge to do everything associated with making the holy things for the Tabernacle. He and his able crew built the very place where our holy God chose to meet with His people. Bezalel created the tent of meeting, the ark of the covenant, the mercy seat, the utensils, the lampstand, the altar of incense, the holy garments for the High Priest, the anointing oil, and on and on.

Bezalel was uniquely gifted as a creative. His creativity knew no bounds. But something else we need to notice: his gifts were anointed by the Holy Spirit of God. He was not a mere technician. He had a true gift for he was supernaturally inspired.

Many years ago I was producing music tracks for a theatrical production. I created the drum tracks, keyboard, bass, and rhythm guitar parts myself. But for one particular song I needed a lead guitar. I don't play lead guitar, so I picked up the phone and called a well-known guitarist in the area. In fact, the man was the town's leading guitar teacher. Surely he could do what I wanted. He came into my studio, plugged in his guitar, listened to the existing track, and then asked, "What do you want me to play?" I froze. What do you mean, "What do I want you to play," I thought to myself. "I'm not the lead guitarist...*you are!*" It was then I realized the difference between a guitarist with a creative gift and a mere technician. This man expertly knew the how-to's of playing a guitar, but he had little to no creative ability flowing out of him. The next time I needed an outside musician, I asked around to make sure the guy could improvise. What a joy to have someone come in with his instrument and experiment with various riffs and runs, asking which ones I, the producer, preferred.

When someone is likewise gifted, there will be an element of anointing to his or her work. I want to take great care here because there may be some of you who will say to yourselves, "Oh, I'm not anointed with any particular genius, so I might as well give up and quit." That would not be a wise conclusion. Why? Not everyone is anointed for everything they do. Even as a creative generalist, there are certain gifts or talents of mine that are stronger than others. Many of them, I do not believe, have any exceptional anointing. But to quit doing them would not be a good steward of the abilities I have been given. After all, Bezalel needed a committee of many craftsmen or technicians who could execute their individual crafts well. He was chosen to be the leader of that group of technicians, and together they were able to realize their collective divine calling. Bezalel, however, carried with him a uniquely ordered leadership anointing in creativity.

Notice also that God intimately knew Bezalel. He described his entire ancestry to Moses and told him in which tribe he could be found. God knew Bezalel because He had prepared him for this work from the moment of conception.

Bezalel would probably have a difficult time of being successful today. After all, he did not self-promote, nor did he suck up to Moses. This may seem like a foolish observation, but self-promotion is the thing we are encouraged to do in our present culture. It's the old saying, "Create a buzz around yourself and people will flock to you." Bezalel did not send out press releases to Moses telling him all he could do for him. Rather, he was more likely hard at work perfecting his many skills in some obscure place. He waited for God to elevate him. No matter how hard that is to do in our culture, it should be our model: perfect our craft, hone our skills, trust God to elevate us in recognition and validation in His timing. "Do you see a man skilful in his work? He will stand before kings; he will not stand before obscure men" (Prov. 22:29).

God knows us as intimately as He knew Bezalel, and He wants us to be able to identify and flow freely in our unique giftings. Like Bezalel, our lives are like seeds, and each seed has a genetic code within it that determines our unique destiny and calling. Unfortunately, there is no quick and easy way to uncover it. There is no fortune cookie that we crack open at age 21 and read, "You are destined to be a _____" Rather, naming our particular seed is a process of discovery.

LESSONS FROM SEEDING

You remember Jesus' parable of the talents in Matthew 13. A

sower went out to sow seed. He sowed with the hope and expectation of reaping a bountiful harvest. Let's say these seeds were pumpkin seeds. Did that sower have the assurance that every seed was destined to be a pumpkin? Yes, because each seed was genetically created to be so. But did he have the assurance that *every* seed would become a pumpkin? Now that is another story.

We know from the parable that every one of those seeds fell into one of four categories: 1) Some of the seeds were immediately eaten by birds. 2) Others fell on rocky ground and sprang up quickly. However, when bad weather hit, their root systems were not well formed, and they withered up and died. 3) Another group of seeds fell on thorny ground and as they began to grow, were choked by weeds and quit growing. 4) The final group of seeds fell on good ground, took root, and became pumpkins.

All of us, of course, want to be in this fourth category. We all want to grow into the fullness of who God genetically made us to be. The reality, however, is that only a small percentage will make it. I don't believe you are reading this book if you were not destined to be in that fourth category. We are not automatically doomed to a fatalistic destiny; rather, our lives are filled with choices. Through the Scriptures, God illumines our way, for His desire is that we do make it, that we do bear fruit that remains.

CONSECRATE YOUR GIFTS

There is an important exhortation we need to heed: "Present your bodies as a living sacrifice, holy and acceptable to God, which is your spiritual worship" (Rom. 12:1). This is especially true for creatives, for our gifts have the potential for bringing us a lot of self-glory. Until we lay them on the altar, they will forever remain our own rather than the Lord's.

One day I was listening to a tape of one of my spiritual mentors, John Sandford, founder of Elijah House and forerunner to the inner healing and deliverance movement. In the tape, he amplified this verse by explaining that as we desire to truly walk with the Lord and yield all that we are to Him, we should hold out to Him everything we know ourselves to be. In other words, put ourselves completely on the altar of sacrifice: our talents, gifts, ambitions, motivational patterns, and ask Him to restore the ones He desires to call forth by the Holy Spirit. This way we can be assured that whatever happens from that moment on, we have yielded our creative gifts to the Creator. Only then can we ever hope to realize Romans 12:2, "Do not be conformed to this world but be transformed by the renewal of your mind, that you may prove what is the will of God, what is good and acceptable and perfect."

Of course we all want our lives to line up in the perfect will of God. To do that, however, requires that everything be yielded to Him, to be molded, renewed, and transformed. These are not things we can do for ourselves. They are done unto us by our Creator, once we have yielded to Him. When we have not yielded but continue to tightly hold onto certain gifts, talents, or ambitious views of ourselves and are afraid to release them with outstretched palms for fear God will take them away or send us on some horrible mission where we don't want to go, we will never realize our destiny. On the other hand, something wonderful happens when a talent or gift is yielded or consecrated on the holy altar: it has the potential of being anointed in God's service, to touch others in a way we could never do otherwise.

CHAPTER 5

Prepare for *Creative Activation* and Growth

Before planting season begins, the ground has to be meticulously prepared. The sod has to be broken up and aerated. It has to be fertilized with the ingredients to provide the seed with the right nutritional and chemical balance. The weeds have to be removed and kept from growing so that the nutrients present in the soil flow only to the all-important seed. Furrows have to be dug, to ensure that the water flows into the new growth rather than away from it. And each seed has to be planted far enough from other ones to give it the optimum chance to take root and grow on its own.

Each of these steps has application in the creative's life. If meticulous care is not given to a pumpkin field, for instance, I can predict with 100% accuracy that the pumpkin crop will not flourish. I can do so because there are laws or principles that govern whether seeds take root or not. In like manner, if you do not properly prepare your personal ground, your personal destiny-bearing seed will not take root and grow freely.

REMOVE THE BITTER ROOTS

There are indeed weeds that spring up from the past that can choke out the life of the healthiest seed. I've seen it happen many times over the years. I'm going to ask you to address the most basic root of all—to examine if you are free to grow.

The cornerstone of the Judeo-Christian heritage is the Ten Commandments, the 10 things God most wants us to heed. Only one of those commandments carries within it a promise, and conversely, a warning. It is the commandment that admonishes:

"Honor your father and your mother, that it will go well with you and that you may enjoy long life on the earth" (Exod. 21:12). The truth is this: if you honor your mother and father, then life will go well with you in the areas in which you honor them. Conversely, if you dishonor your mother or father by conscious or unconscious judgments in any way, then it will not go well with you in these areas.

I cannot explain exactly how this is true. I just know that it is. It is one of the divine Laws to which we are each accountable. I have seen many lives destroyed because this commandment was not heeded. But before I point fingers at anyone else's life, I will share something of my own, and how it affected my creative growth.

My mother died when I was 25. I was angry with God because he took the wrong parent. He left me with the one I didn't like—my father. He was in World War II when I was born, and I didn't even know he existed until I was nine months old. For nine months, I was the center of attention for my mother, grandmother and two aunts. Then he arrived. I hated him from day one.

Our relationship was rocky throughout my life. He and Mother were not particularly close. There were old wounds and she passed her feelings onto me. Never once during my growing up years did I feel close to him, did I look up to him, or did I honor him as my father. In my heart, I judged him in many ways and harbored silent criticisms of him. Then my mother died.

It would require another book to detail our father-daughter transformation, but it did occur. And the relationship we have now is glorious. I learned the truth and power behind that commandment. I could never succeed at anything I was meant to do if I harbored the wrong spirit toward either of my parents. But it took work. It took sincere repentance on my part for judging and dishonoring my father. It took asking his forgiveness for pulling away and refusing to let him be a father to me. It took time. It took tears. It took confession.

There may be some of you who say, "But you don't know how horrible my father (or mother) was. He abused me, or beat me, or abandoned me." I can only tell you what I know: God's Word is God's Word. He holds your parents accountable for their actions toward you. And He holds you accountable for being obedient to His commandments and honoring them. I have heard many stories of people whose lives have been re-directed once they confessed their hatred or bitterness or judgment of their parents. It's an act of laying it down and letting Him sort out the hurts, the blame, and impart forgiveness and healing.

There was a time in my early creative life where my inner motivation was, "I'll show that man what I can do." God did not bless my efforts. He couldn't do so and still remain true to His commandment. Once our relationship was healed, however, my father has become my greatest champion, proud of me whether I am a known success or not. Having his blessing has made all the difference in the world in my creative journey. Once the bitter roots were removed, I could move on to cultivating the ground.

CULTIVATE THE GROUND

It takes time to properly cultivate the ground for a seed to take root. For creatives, waiting for their big idea or vision, there are some things we can do to help ourselves on the journey. When I was involved in my *Artist's Way* support group, our leader, Sarah Tinnon, gave us a unique project. She assigned us a "media deprivation week" and for seven whole days until we met again, we were not allowed to listen to TV or radio, read a newspaper, go on-line, or attend a movie. Nada. I thought to myself, "This is going to be a cinch, because as I've mentioned before, I normally live in a world of quiet." What was enlightening to me, however, was that when our group of seven (writers, actors, directors, cartoonists) met the next week, they were overflowing with enthusiasm. They were amazed at how freely ideas came to them throughout the week and had never before seen the value of quiet for the creative.

For many years, music was no longer a part of my day-to-day life. As a songwriter, I concluded I had failed because I could not make money as a writer. When my husband died, I could not sing or play the piano for a long time because I became too emotional.

I had never been a choir person, not because I wanted the spot-light, but in reality because I don't read music that well. I write and sing by ear, which doesn't bode well for an alto trying to follow a part. Nonetheless, it came time when I longed to express myself musically again and being inconspicuous in the middle row of the choir suited my mood. We performed a glorious Christmas concert, complete with a live orchestra, and my spirit was overflowing. I honestly surprised myself by how much I had missed music.

Several other experiences followed, wherein I began to lend my musical talents for the benefit of others rather than myself. I encouraged a man to record one of my songs as a gift to his wife for their 51st anniversary. Alan has a marvelous bass voice and had sung for years with the Robert Shaw Chorale. At 77, he rarely sang anymore, and I had this brainstorm to encourage his talents and enable them to live on as a special memory for his family. It was a song I had written 15 years earlier, but when I played it for him, he exclaimed, "I can't believe it—it's as if you wrote it just for Mimi and me." Knowing how I've always been ahead of schedule, I just smiled and said, "I did." I earned absolutely no money from this gesture, but I earned far more. I re-learned the joy that my musical talent could bring others when it is freely given with no thought of receiving anything in return.

One particular evening I was playing the piano and had a deep inner knowing that I was being taught something important. For years I held my music as a right, a thing that deserved money, praise, or recognition. When I tried to pitch it, shop it, market it, and sell it, I lost the heart and soul of it. I thought of the woman who brought her costly ointment to Jesus and poured it on His feet and realized how precious are the gifts we have been given. Like her bottle of ointment, they often have to be broken in order to be used—poured out in sacrificial giving to others—for them to have true worth, giving them back to the Lord with no thought of holding onto them or getting something for ourselves. Success guru Napoleon Hill refers to this principle as the "Law of Compensation," which he discovered in an essay by Ralph Waldo Emerson.

The Law of Compensation can work for you or against you depending upon the way you guide it. It may take many years for punishment to follow transgression or for reward to follow virtue, but the compensation always will find you out.[4]

We are called to be stewards of every gift we have been given. A steward is not an owner. Rather, a steward has been entrusted with something belonging to the master, and he is judged by how well he has fulfilled his responsibilities.

If your creativity falls in the area of writing or conceptual ideas, you will enjoy Bill Backer's book *The Care And Feeding of Basic Ideas*. Backer is the advertising genius behind such campaigns as Coke's "I Want To Teach The World To Sing," and Miller Beer's "It's Miller Time," among others. A conceptualizer whom I admire greatly, Backer agrees wholeheartedly with the concept of stewardship responsibility toward one's ideas or talents. He says we are given ideas to properly nurture and birth, and if we are slack in that stewardship, the great ideas will be given to someone else.

Take Stephen Spielberg. Have you ever wondered why he seems to get all the great movies to do? I believe it's because he's been a faithful steward of those movie ideas he was given, and as a reward, he was given more. He took the ideas given him and did the painstaking work necessary to bring them to the screen. He's been rewarded for it.

CREATIVE SURVIVAL SKILLS OF OUR FOREFATHERS

There is great wisdom studying the Israelites' early agricultural way of life, which Jesus heavily drew upon in giving us the parable of the sower and the seed. If we are to earn our living through our gifts and talents, then we need to view these gifts as creative seeds. Many lessons on sowing and reaping creative seeds can be gleaned from our forefathers.

When early civilizations first began to sow seed, they had no idea whether they were sowing into good ground. They had to learn through trial and error. In other words, they would scatter seed everywhere. As the seed began to sprout, they observed where the areas of greatest fertility seemed to be, and the next time they sowed, they would go to those exact locations. The principle is vital to the creative. We throw out our ideas and try any number of things. That's all well and good. But take special note what areas are producing growth and sow your next efforts there.

Sow a variety of seeds. Our forefathers did not live on just one type of seed. Rather, they instinctively knew their bodies needed variety in order to survive. They were always busy sowing or reaping something, and preparing for the next season. We should do the same in sowing our creative seeds—sow into many different areas of our lives, not just holding out for one thing. If all they depended upon were lentils to sustain them, they would have starved the rest of the year.

The origin of stewardship. The principle of stewardship was developed when nobles took over the land from the original farmers. Over time, the people had no sense of proprietorship or pride in their work. God began to address this issue through the prophets of the time, and revival was born. For example, Nehemiah forced a return of property to the original owners after a certain length of time (Neh. 5). This confirms the principle I mentioned earlier about the necessity of the shepherding role toward what we create. Business leaders would do well to keep this principle in mind. When they see creative ideas coming from within their company, place the idea's creator in charge of shepherding the process. If you take it and turn it over to someone in middle management to shepherd, I can almost with certainty predict the idea will never bear the fruit that it was intended to bear. Wed the creative with his creation and surround that emotional bond with all the corporate support you can give. Such is the key to unlocking creative power within your corporate framework.

Continue planting the same seeds. Crops become more stable the more those seeds are planted. This is an encouraging promise to those of us who have planted creative seeds (such as my musical), only to see them flounder or derail for a season. We too easily conclude, "Well, that doesn't work. Let's try something else." No, the converse is true. Continue planting those same seeds, for they strengthen and multiply more over time.

How to plow. When Jesus said, "No one who puts his hand to the plow and looks back is fit for the kingdom of God," He was revealing many key insights (Luke 9:62). The early plows were light and only scratched three or four inches below the surface. Jesus' admonition wasn't to warn them to plow in a straight line. Rather, it was because the sower (of whatever seed) needed all of his concentration so he could push down hard and dig deep enough into the ground. Plowing the ground for our creative seeds is very hard work and needs tremendous concentration and energy.

Vary the order of sowing to ensure survival. The wheat was sown first, then the barley. That was because the wheat took much longer to grow, and thus was of far more value to the farmer. Barley was important because it grew very quickly, and the harvest was easy. Thus, while he was waiting to harvest the slower-growing wheat, the farmer was still able to survive through his barley crop. The variety always kept food on the table. A creative instinctively knows which projects are the slower-growing ones. It will likely take a long time for huge projects like musicals, films, and TV series to produce harvest. Thus, if I spend all my efforts there and there alone, I will most likely be doomed to starvation and extinction.

Watch for signs of harvest. When the spring rains came, the water caused the grains to swell. The wise farmer kept a watchful eye on his crop to see when the seedling stage was past. When the crop was time to be harvested, the grain became tinder dry. During this stage, there was the ever-present danger of fire. The farmer thus needed to be extremely diligent, even sleeping out in the field, to protect his crop from ruination until it was time to harvest. Again, as creatives, we need to keep ever-watchful eyes on our creative seeds, and notice signs when those seeds are moving into different stages.

Remember the poor. God's heart is always for the poor and needy, and the farmers' was to be likewise. Therefore, God instructed him to leave the corners of the fields for the poor, and during the harvest, to leave some of the produce on the ground for the poor to be able to glean.

Don't muzzle the ox. It was important that the ox had the freedom to enjoy the fruit of its labor. God's heart is for the beast as well as the farmer. Such a practice created a bond of respect between owner and worker, and that bond produced greater productivity. This is an important principle for creatives and business owners. The absolute worst thing businesses can do is to strip creative ideas from people and not allow them to share in the rewards. In other words, if your employee invents something, and you pay him a salary, a common practice of today is to view that idea as a "work for hire." As the company enriches itself, the creator of that idea begins to feel devalued and deprived. God's way is to let it be known that your company rewards ingenuity and creativity, and that over and above their salary, creatives will receive fruit from their creative labor in the form of some profit participation or royalty.

Appreciate the value of threshing, winnowing, and sifting. Threshing is separating the grain from the straw. The first step involved beating the grain with a flail or long flexible stick. Often oxen were used to trample the grain with their hooves. In fact, the meaning of the Hebrew word for "thresh" is "to trample." During this process, the oxen enjoyed some of the grain. Next came the winnowing process, which involved throwing the mixture of grain and straw into the air. The heavier grain fell to the ground, whereas the straw was blown away. The chaff was used to fire the stoves, the straw used to feed the animals, and the grain—that which was of greatest value for man's survival—remained. Notice that nothing in God's economy went to waste. Thus, if you find yourself throwing something away, perhaps within it lies a creative seed whereby you can make good use of that very thing. In other words, look for the opportunity in what is being discarded.

The final stage was sifting, which in essence was the purifying process. Nothing passed through sifting except the grain itself. It was important that the farmer watch out for and remove any darnels (i.e., tares) at this stage. Darnels looks identical to wheat until the grain ripens, when it becomes black instead of yellow. These grains are bitter and cause sickness when eaten. Jesus' exhortation "you will know them by their fruits" now becomes more meaningful. We need to be very discerning and remove those things from our work that is not the purest essence of what we were meant to plant and reap.

Don't forget to store. The farmer's final step was to store the grain in receptacles. These were clay jars, pits, or cisterns, or a room attached to the house or a barn. Entire cities often had silos or granaries. Storehouses were built of brick in order to keep the pests away. There were two primary reasons for storage: to support the family or town in the days to come, and also to hold the offering that was to be given to the Lord. As creatives we need to also think about how the Lord desires us to set aside the harvest when it comes, how we can safeguard it for our future survival needs, as well as ensure that which we are to give to support the Lord's work. All too often, we have a tendency to plant seeds in one area and turn our backs because we're now involved in something in another area. He blesses our efforts when we take great care in watching over our harvest and develop plans for storage and distribution to the needs of others.

Always give thanks. When God promises to give us our daily bread, He means for us to work alongside of Him in producing that loaf. The work is hard. There are many steps, and many things to learn about successful creative seed-sowing. We aren't to sit back and wait for someone else to do all the work. Rather, He desires to instruct us how to produce the grain, which produces the bread. That's why when we finally place our figurative "loaf" in front of us to reap the salivary reward, we are to give thanks. After all, thankfulness should be the natural result of all the painstakingly hard work it took to produce that loaf![5]

OTHER WAYS TO PRODUCE CREATIVE FRUIT

The above section had a great deal to do with showing us specific how-to's as they relate to sowing creative seed. But there is more to consider when it comes to the choices we make. The Scriptures teach us to "work out your own salvation with fear and trembling" (Phil. 2:12). We need to fill up our daily quotient of time in ways that will enrich the seed of our creativity: such as through quiet times spent with the Lord, filing ideas that come, practicing and honing our craft, and using our gifts for the betterment of others. There is simply no easy way to produce fruit other than by effort.

The benefit of journaling. Julia Cameron discusses this practice at length in *The Artist's Way.* Set time each morning before your time with the Lord to drain your brain of the kinetic thoughts that are going nowhere. These times are not designed to be exercises in literary genius. Rather, they are designed to rid your mind of the static thoughts that are taking up valuable space on your mental hard drive. Until we do this, we cannot make room for new ideas and thoughts that await us.

Keep in touch with the industry you desire to be part of. When I began my entertainment development company in 1994, I knew absolutely nothing about the way the industry did business. To become credible as a screenwriter took a great deal of both time and money. The first thing I did was to establish my entertainment corporation and from that business entity, I conducted business. I subscribed to popular trade publications such as *Hollywood Reporter*, the *BluBook Film, TV, and Video Resource Directory*, and the *Hollywood Creative Directory*, and read them diligently. I made it my business to know who the key decision-makers were, what types of projects they were looking for, and what current trends were unfolding.

Concurrently, I spent time each day working on my screenwriting craft. I couldn't very well pitch projects if I had nothing to pitch. But even before I could begin doing that, I attended screenwriting seminars and studied how-to books on screenwriting. I hired writing coaches to advise me on project development and polishing techniques. All of these efforts were essential to learning my craft.

I'll never forget the day I began to see these efforts pay off. In 1995, I was working in my studio in Gainesville, Georgia, and the phone rang. It was the late TV wunderkind Brandon Tartikoff asking to see one of the company's projects. I began to sweat. Here it was—potential payoff time—could I carry on a professional conversation or come across like a bumbling idiot? Fortunately I kept my starstruck excitement in check, and I conducted business with this entertainment titan. With regained confidence, I continued pitching my projects to production companies in Hollywood and soon attracted the attention of such companies as ABC, NBC, Hearst Entertainment, MCA-TV, Universal, Disney, and 20th Century Fox. It takes great effort and time to become credible in a new industry.

I followed the same procedure back in the late 70s and early 80s when I was learning the songwriting craft. There frankly is no other way. It's all part of "paying one's dues." We may be born with gifts, but the how-to expression of those gifts develops only over time, with much practice. And the chosen industry's acceptance of us—which the Scriptures calls "favor with man"—takes even longer.

Be open to advice from others. When I taught songwriting, invariably someone would come up and say, "Would you listen to my song? God gave it to me." I would cringe inside, because I always knew what was coming. Sure enough, I would listen and the song would be horrendous. This is an important concept to grasp because while God may have truly given the inspiration, He expects us to master the modern-day expression of the artform.

Allow me to use a songwriting example, since it is a shorter and more compact creative discipline. Why would God inspire someone to write a song that had no chance of communicating to listeners? Now, perhaps He is the only One who wants to hear it, but more often than not, He gives us gifts to communicate with others. He delights in using us in the lives of other people. Key to this communicative process is learning to say something in a way the intended recipient can receive it. The original idea of the fledgling songwriter may well be inspired, but if it is delivered in a form that prevents it from being received well, then the gift is not fully realized. If I try to give instruction to the songwriter how to improve her song and she retorts with, "No, that's not how God gave it to me. I'm not going to change anything," then most likely she will never grow nor be received in her songwriting gift. She truly may have one, but it will remain unpolished and undisciplined.

RELEASE YOUR INNER CHILD

After reading the first draft of my book, a new acquaintance admitted that she was unable to do one of the self-reflecting exercises. I pondered for a moment and then asked her, "Were you always the 'little adult' growing up?" She was astounded, and asked, "How did you know?"

My mother was an alcoholic, and for most of my childhood, I filled in as the role of her caretaker, the one who would emotionally buoy her when she sunk into depression. I didn't have the freedom to fling myself into her lap at all times of the day and say, "Mama, I'm the child here...not you." What happened was this little girl part of me splintered off. Whenever she would rise up, I wouldn't know what to do with her. I was terrified of her fears, her insecurities, and her loneliness. I couldn't face them in any other way than to stuff them back down. The result was that though I gave the appearance of having it all together, I was a half-person. Until I tapped into that little girl part of me—the one who dreams and longs and imagines—my gifts could not truly flow as God intended.

One of Jesus' greatest discourses on the kingdom of heaven involved a child.

And calling to him a child, he put him in the midst of them, and said, "Truly, I say to you, unless you turn and become like children, you will never enter the kingdom of heaven" (Matt. 18:2-3).

There is truly a realm in our spiritual journey with the heavenly Father that we will never enter except we become like children. That's what Jesus is saying. When we were children, we trusted completely. Our hearts hadn't scabbed over through years of hurt, disappointment, anger, abuse, or rejection. When we come to God and want to follow Him, those scabs and scars are still there. As we experience new life, He begins to point out things that need to be relinquished, such as anger and unforgiveness. He often reveals memories that need a healing touch that only He can give. When He points to a place deep that we have kept under lock and key for years, He does so because He wants this inner child to be set free. He wants us to literally invite Him into those places to heal us.

"Now the Lord is the Spirit, and where the Spirit of the Lord is, there is freedom" (2 Cor. 3:17). Freedom is His goal for us—our inner freedom so that little child within us can be fully integrated with the adult that we are becoming. As that union develops, we experience creative freedom we have never before known. However, in all honesty, this is a part of the journey we often avoid, because it can be painful. It's not easy to re-live painful memories, yet as the psalmist says, "You desire truth in the inward being; therefore teach me wisdom in my secret heart" (Ps. 51:6).

In the normal course of our lives, we often are confronted with internal blocks. We may not know what the block is or what to do about it, but we know intuitively that something is amiss. I hit one of those blocks a few years after my first husband left me, and I began dating Mike. Quite frankly, my emotional life went haywire. One minute I thought I was falling in love; the next minute, I was terrified and everything inside of me made me want to run. I was a mess. Poor Mike. He had no clue what to do with me, whether from one minute to the next I would be hot or cold. I was helpless to do anything about it. We even made a joke about it and made up a name for "it"—a "freak-out." No amount of prayer resolved it. Months and months went by, and it became obvious that I was emotionally crippled. That's when I was forced to make a choice: Was I going to to face the pain and seek help, or was I going to remain in that "unfree," bound state?

I chose to get help. I'll never forget one particular therapy session with me, Mike, and the counselor. During the session, my counselor gently triggered a memory that had been lodged there since childhood. I didn't "see" the memory intellectually. I "felt" the memory and began to sob uncontrollably. The two of them were speechless, because they both knew me as someone typically very controlled and "together." Suddenly those emotions were released with the force of a dam breaking for what seemed an eternity. Though painful at the time, the experience unlocked an internal mystery to me and was key to opening the door and releasing me from internal bondage.

Invite God into the memory. Most of us facing internal blocks need the assistance of someone gifted and trained in inner healing. Margaret was 49 years old and found herself in a counselor's office because she was miserable and wanted to die. She was lonely, overweight, and had zero self-worth. Skillfully, he began to tap into a key childhood memory. When Margaret was nine years old, she was habitually late to class, so one day the teacher decided to teach Margaret a lesson. That day when Margaret came in, late as usual, the teacher had the children each come to the blackboard and write a sentence describing her. Margaret was forced to sit there in horror watching the sentences appear: "Margaret is fat." "Margaret is ugly." "Margaret is not worth anything." Sure enough, over time,

Margaret became every one of those things, like a self-fulfilling prophecy.

The counselor then had Margaret close her eyes and revisit that painful memory. He said, "You forgot someone. Do you see God?" She struggled slightly with his meaning, then realized that if God never leaves us, where was He? He said, "Ask Him to show Himself to you in this memory." With eyes still closed, she prayed and asked God to show Himself to her. Suddenly she saw Him. The counselor asked, "What is He doing?" With tears running down her face, Margaret said, "He walked up to the front and erased the sentences and wrote, 'Margaret is worthy,' 'Margaret is loved.'"

One of the areas of greatest need among creatives is learning how to become as children. It is a very important journey into wholeness, and an important part of our Creativity Training Workshops.

CHAPTER 6

Name Your Seed

I magine yourself standing before your plot of ground. You've tilled the soil, made the furrows, weeded, fertilized, watered, and now you are ready to plant. This is a critical stage, and believe it or not, in a creative sense, you have to know what it is you are planting. I'm not trying to be facetious. Here you are, holding out a seed to put in the ground. What is it? If you *know*, then everything you do from here on out will produce what you want to produce. Why? Because you know what the seed is. If it is a pumpkin seed, you can have complete faith that with proper watering and weeding, in a matter of weeks, you will have a pumpkin. That's the "Law of Applied Faith," which we'll discuss at length in Chapter 12.

"Naming your seed" is key to your creative journey. Chances are, the most difficult part of this journey may be here. You look at the seed, which is symbolic of your life, and you ask yourself, "So...what is it?"

It's not simple, however. The process of discerning fully who we are is a *process*. Throughout life, we glean insights that magnify and delineate our specific areas of gifts, talents, and abilities. All these insights are important to embrace, for they help to round out our understanding of who we are. In 1975, I was convinced I was to be a songwriter. That's it...a songwriter, nothing else. Later, in 1986, that self-awareness grew when I wrote *A Time To Dance*. Suddenly, I wasn't just a songwriter, I was a composer/playwright. The point I want to stress here is that "naming your seed" is not usually a one-time event. Rather, most likely you will arrive at several key life junctions where your individual "name" becomes even more delineated with its kingdom, phylum, class, order, family, genus, and species.

DISCOVER YOUR MOTIVATIONAL PATTERN

A motivational pattern is different from a talent or a gift, but understanding it is key to operating freely in your gifting. It is an internal set of motivations through which we each operate. For example, one songwriter may be motivated by the chance to earn millions of dollars, whereas another songwriter may be motivated more by the creative challenge of writing songs for a particular recording artist or to reach a particular audience with a life-changing message. The songwriting itself is the same gift, but the motivations are quite different.

I discovered my motivational patterns quite by accident. I've already said that since 1975 I believed my "call" was to be a songwriter, and by 1983 I was one. I had two publishers who were actively behind my development as a writer and pitching my songs to record producers. I was writing with top writers and being mentored by the man who shepherded the career of one of my favorite songwriters, Mac Davis. When my son Tyler was born, and I was unable to commute to Nashville any longer, the door was nonetheless wide open for me to continue to submit my songs and work long distance with other writers. I was at "the top of my game." But I was immensely depressed.

I want to pause here and exhort my fellow creatives concerning an important truth: when you reach a point of depression, it is often a signpost that something is amiss. If we medicate that depression or drown it out with alcohol, we might miss a vital insight concerning our journeys.

I had it all: a husband whose financial support paid the bills, so all I had to do was write, demo my songs, and submit them to my publishers. But I was miserable. I did what I have learned to do over the years: when I reach an emotional impasse, I stop and wait for clarification.

Tyler was an infant and slept a lot. While he slept, I made a conscious decision—again, one of those "choices in life"—to seek the Lord and ask for clarity as to why I was doing what I thought I was supposed to do and finding myself depressed. During his every nap, I was out on the porch reading, journalling, and praying. It was one of those "dark nights of the soul." Not very glamorous, but very real that lasted six months.

One day, a friend of mine gave me a book by Ralph Mattson and Arthur Miller, *Finding A Job You Can Love*, that shed light on the answer. The book's thrust was a scientific study showing that once a person finds the motivational pattern or patterns of his life, he will never stray from them. Even if a person knows nothing of such patterns, his eventual work choices will reflect those patterns, and regardless of circumstances, that person will be 100% true to his innate pattern. 100%? That caught my attention. Of course, what the authors suggest is that the earlier a person understands exactly what motivates him, the better his chances are for a rewarding and enriching life's work.

Motivational patterns are threads that run throughout our lives. To uncover them takes time, reflection, and analysis. What I learned in my self-analysis has proved life-changing and has been an important signpost in discerning "the next step" along my journey.

THE TEST

You may test yourself to determine your motivational pattern, but I highly recommend partnering with someone who knows you well. It is also helpful if that person has analytical thinking skills, for your partner will help you to dig deeper to answer your questions rather than get by with a pat answer. You can, of course, do this test alone if critical thinking skills are in your giftings palette, and you are able to look objectively at your own life.

The test is relatively simple.

Divide your life into age segments (0-6, grade school, middle school, high school, college, 20-30, 30-40, etc.) and use a different sheet of paper for each age bracket.

Ask yourself two questions and write out the answers for each of these age periods: Name two things you enjoyed doing during this period. And name two things other people said you were good at.[6]

The answers need to be as specific as possible. For instance, if you liked playing with dolls when you were young, what did you like about that? Was it acting out scenes between the dolls? Was it designing outfits for them? Was it orchestrating playtime with the neighbors? Be as specific as you can. Your partner will be key here to encourage you to describe the memories, ask deeper exploratory questions, and write down the motivations that come to mind. Soon, the patterns begin to surface. When they do, look back over your life and see if those patterns have appeared consistently in those activities you excelled in and were missing in those activities which produced feelings of dissatisfaction. This is how we determine a true motivational pattern: *it will appear consistently throughout the happiest memories of our lives.* It makes sense that we are happiest at the times we are most highly motivated, and miserable when those motivations are stifled.

When I initially read this test, I thought, "This is ridiculous. I don't need to do this, I already know my common thread. I need to have a creative outlet." Fortunately, I forced myself to complete the entire exercise. I encourage you to do the same. Sure enough, in every age segment, I was most fulfilled when I was doing something creative. Also, those were the areas wherein I received 100% of my commendations from others. What I had failed to see, however, was a secondary motivation that began to surface: in *every* period, I was most fulfilled when I had an element of creative control. Bingo. Suddenly, I became aware why I was depressed.

As a songwriter, I was most motivated at the inception of the initial idea for the song and the musical expression of it. However, in my current situation—a young mother needing to stay home with her child—I could not travel to Nashville and have an active input in my writing career. Rather, I sent my songs off to someone else to follow through with, or "shepherd" them. My personal motivational pattern was therefore high during the creation of the song and recording the demo. However, when I sent it to a publisher, I let loose of the creative controls, and for the most part, my songs remained in boxed reels on his shelf. That's when my motivation died. My present set of circumstances prevented my shepherding my own creation, and my depression, therefore, became a very important signpost to alert me that my motivational pattern was being ignored.

Realize, though, that this is my motivational pattern. It's not everyone's in this same situation, for there are many successful writers who do very well in a long distance relationship with their publishers. I was not to be one of them.

Understanding my own God-given motivations has been liberating and has been the cornerstone for many creative decisions I have since made. The first decision was to quit the commute-mentality to Nashville. Instead, I invested an inheritance in setting up my own recording studio so that I could learn to produce by myself and be less dependent upon a publisher to demo my material. I turned my back on Nashville and devoted myself full-time to my advertising agency, which I expanded, reasoning that though I may never have Kenny Rogers' next hit, I could at least have creative control over commercials and ad campaigns I would create for my clients. That decision paid off. Since 1986 I have been able to support myself and my art through my advertising work, and have found a measure of fulfillment using creativity to help businesses succeed.

From that moment on, anytime I need to make a decision as to my future, I always check it against my motivational pattern to see if it lines up. When the opportunity presented itself to produce my musical, it was a no-brainer. Talk about creative control! I would have to create everything: the script, the music, the P.R. materials, and the business plan. Earlier on, during my self-analysis, I had learned that in those sets of circumstances where my creativity envelope was stretched to the limit.

KNOW YOURSELF

The apostle Paul said,

I bid every one among you not to think of himself more highly than he ought to think, but to think with sober judgment, each according to the measure of faith which God has assigned him (Rom. 12:3).

This is a critical verse for creatives. Notice God's Word exhorts us to self-reflect and discern the abilities we've been given. We've all smiled when someone asks a little child, "What do you want to be when you grow up?" and he says, "I'm going to be President of the United States." But as that child matures, so should his inner beacon. God gives to each one of us a "measure of faith" tied to our assigned destiny. When you look at the seed (your life), God wants you to know exactly what it is, and what it will become.

In early 1999, my husband Mike had just died, and I felt directed to start a film production company in L.A. In a matter of weeks, all the doors shut and plans fell through. I didn't know who I was anymore, or what I was to do. I was in Florida visiting my father at the time, and once again he gave me tapes by Napoleon Hill to listen to. Why on earth I resisted his suggestions I will never know, but I did. Year after year he would try to advise me, and time and again I would dismiss his advice without hesitation. This time, though, I was a whipped puppy. With my husband gone, I seemed to have no bearings for the rest of my life.

Driving back to Georgia, I popped in Hill's tape of his bestselling book *Think and Grow Rich* and prepared to roll my eyes in disdain. Suddenly here was this man—long dead—who nailed my biggest problem within the first 10 minutes of the tape. His thesis was: "Whatsoever the mind of man can conceive, the mind of man can achieve."[7] The secret lay in the winnowing away of everything but the primary desire (i.e., looking at the seed and calling it by name).

I went to the Scriptures to check out Hill's philosophy. It was there: "God is at work in you, both to will [put desire in] and to work for His good pleasure" (Phil. 2:13). "May He grant you your heart's desire and fulfill all your plans" (Ps. 20:4). When Solomon was king of Israel, God blessed him as he built all that he desired. "It is God's gift to man that every one should eat and drink and take pleasure in all his work" (Eccl. 3:13). The truth is that the closer we are aligned with our Creator, His desires for us become our desires, which makes it okay to follow our heart's desire. In fact, it's more than okay. It's what pleases God most.

I then asked myself: What is it you really want to do? Not what you should do...or what others have always told you that you should do...or what you should do if you want to earn a lot of money...or what you should do to please certain people in your life. But what is it you really desire? Suddenly, I knew the core of my problem. I enjoyed doing a lot of things, but I had not yet clarified my desire. Since that were true, it stood to reason I would never get there. A car that doesn't know where it's going will get there every time.

By this time, I had already weeded out a lot of things and concluded that I was a writer, but what did that mean? What did I desire to do as a writer? Did that conclusion line up with the motivational pattern I had discovered for myself? Was I going to be content writing screenplay after screenplay and pitching them to some unknown company in La La Land, hoping against hope that somebody would pick one up and say, "Now, this is one great script. I'm going to do all the hard stuff now and produce it." Right. But that's honestly what I thought, or at least hoped.

Something clearly was out of line. I knew I was a writer. But to give over creative control to some nameless person? To expect someone else to shepherd my work? I had learned better. As I pondered this question, the inner voice said, "Produce your work yourself." For months I tried to talk myself out of it, throwing out every self-limitation I could think of: I don't have name recognition; I don't have the money; nobody would think me credible enough to give me money; and I wouldn't know how to begin. The list went on and on to such an extent it's a wonder I was even capable of getting out of the bed in the mornings.

Ironically, at about the same time blues-singing sensation Francine Reed and Ted Moore, her business manager, read my musical and wanted to be involved with its production, I had already reached the conclusion that my personal creative path was leading me toward producing my own work. Thus, in 1999 my thinking had finally crystallized to actually verbalize my desire: to be a writer/producer, with *A Time To Dance* becoming the first project under my entertainment development company.

I even went so far as to write out a personal mission statement, which was to write and produce projects that inspire people toward positive change. Arriving at this level of self-knowledge took many, many years.

HOW TO KNOW WHEN YOU FIND IT

Narrowing down your basic desire takes time. You may be lucky. I know people who have known all their lives what they wanted to do, and they're doing it. But most of us get bogged down in the mire of the self-reflective process.

The steps to take are these:
1. Rid yourself of any bitter root.
2. Spend regular time each day with God, asking His direction and reading His Word.
3. Journal your thoughts.
4. Ask those who know you well what they could see you most doing.
5. Work through the motivational pattern exercise.
6. Access the options that present themselves in your life.
7. Write down the pros and cons of each of those options.
8. As you move forward in the most apparent direction, look for signs of confirmation.

CHAPTER 7

Dreams and Visions

God speaks to us in many ways. The longer I walk with Him, the more magnificently He speaks. As soon as I've neatly placed Him in one box, wherein I'm comfortable hearing Him this way, He does something entirely new. Then there are those times when we are absolutely certain God has been leading us to do something, and we wind up flat on our faces, crying out, "Lord, did I hear You at all?" I find comfort in Hebrews 5:14 which explains that we learn by practice to distinguish good from evil. That's what life is: learning to hear God's voice, for our creative gifts are fully realized only when they are channeled within the flow of His current.

I would be remiss if I did not touch upon how God may speak to someone through dreams or visions, for these revelatory lines of communication comprise a third of Scripture. Moreover, every major turning point in the history of God's dealings with His people involved dreams.

I believe that creatives are uniquely wired to receive such divine communication, for we are prophetic by nature, attuned to spiritual things by design. We are created with "ears to hear." Einstein's theory of relativity came to him in a dream. The sewing machine was seen in a dream, and thus invented, as was the telegraph by Samuel Morse. Dreams also were responsible for Handel's "Messiah," Paul McCartney's "Yesterday," and the Mamas and Papas' hit, "California Dreamin'."

The Lord explained to Miriam, Aaron, and Moses in Numbers 12:6-8 that He speaks to prophets (i.e., those equipped or wired to "hear" God) in one of five ways: in a dream, a vision, dark speech, mouth to mouth, or face to face. Jesus often spoke in parables, in dark sayings filled with symbols and analogies. If you think about it, this means of communication is very Eastern. Whereas we Westerners speak assertively and often "in your face," people in the Far East speak indirectly. Discourse to them is more polite and waits to be received by the listener. In like manner, our Lord often speaks to us in symbols and visual pictures, waiting for us to ask for more, never assuming and just pouring it all into our minds. If we truly seek enlightenment and clarification, it will come.

Our early church fathers highly regarded the belief that God speaks in dreams. Polycarp (AD 69-155) was Bishop of Smyrna, a disciple of the Apostle John. He dreamed that he would be killed in Rome, and he was. (Remember, one of the jobs of the Holy Spirit is to declare to us the things to come, as stated in John 16:13.) Tertullian of Carthage (AD 160-220) wrote, "Almost the greater part of mankind derive their knowledge of God from dreams." Irenaeus, the Bishop of Gaul in AD 200 believed dreams were a way for him to maintain proper contact with God. Cyprian, Bishop of Carthage in AD 258 used his dreams to gain practical guidance in making daily decisions. Augustine (AD 354-430) listed several of his dreams in his writings and declared they were an important way in which God spoke to mankind, and Jerome (AD 340-420), who translated the Latin Bible, was converted as a secular scholar to Christianity by a dream.

How dark our days became in Western culture with the Greek mindset of Aristotle, the philosopher who maintained that anything not tangible and logical is irrelevant. Thomas Aquinas, before the Reformation, promoted the belief that people only can know truth through reason and the five sensory perceptions. Even our International Standard Bible Dictionary asserts the following: "To accept the ability to receive knowledge or truth by way of extra-sensory perception in visions and dreams is simply psychotic or neurotic at best." How incredibly tragic that our so-called "age of enlightenment" plunged our generation into spiritual darkness, turning a deaf ear to God's revelatory voice.

Kings of every nation once searched the world over to find men and women gifted in hearing from God and interpreting their dreams. I see a new movement occurring, however, where God is pouring out His heart through dreams and visions, as if to wake up His slumbering people: "Behold, I'm doing a new thing...do you not perceive it?" (Isaiah 43:19) People are experiencing revelatory messages now in record numbers. We are living, I believe, in the most revelatory time in all of history—the time prophesied in the book of Joel—when God pours out His Spirit on all mankind, and men and women see dreams and visions (Joel 2:28).

My purpose here is not to debate whether dreams and visions truly exist. Rather, I want to challenge my fellow creatives to be open to receiving illumination from God Himself on this subject. For more in-depth reading, I refer readers to John and Paula Sandford's classic, *The Elijah Task*. Additionally, John Paul Jackson's entire ministry, Streams Ministries, which is accessible on-line at www.streamsministries.com, is devoted almost exclusively to dreams and the Hebraic method of dream interpretation.

There is much God longs to communicate to His people, if only we had ears to hear. Not long after a devastating experience in my creative journey (discussed at length in a later chapter), I had a strange dream. Actually, there were a series of dreams all dealing with the same theme. In this one particular dream, however, there were two dead cats floating in my toilet. One was full grown; the other appeared stillborn. It was a chilling sight. The water was swirling around in the toilet, for I was flushing them away. Just as they were about to vanish down the bowl, the larger cat's head lifted up. It was not dead! I woke up. I had the sense this was a significant dream for me and remained puzzled for many days, asking the Lord, "What does this mean? What are You trying to say to me?" Some weeks passed and I was playing the piano, which often soothes me and releases feelings that need expressing. Suddenly, in the midst of one particular song, the image of the cats swirling around the toilet flashed in my mind, and the Lord spoke to my heart, "You thought your music was dead, and you were ready to flush it out of your life. Look at it...it is still alive." Tears flowed down my cheeks as hope was rekindled inside of me. He used a dream to confirm what others had been telling me following the premiere of my musical, which ended in financial devastation: "Don't give up. Your music is not dead."

There had been a particular film idea I had been thinking about off and on for years. It was actually a very personal story, one that would allow me to vent all the feelings I went through during my divorce. Needless to say, it was a revenge-tragedy kind of story that I titled *Retribution!* It sat in my file for months. One day, I had a breakthrough. As I've mentioned before, I try to begin each day spending time in prayer and Scripture reading. This day was like every other day. I gave the Lord my mind, heart, talents, abilities, and asked Him to teach me what He wanted me to learn that day. The moment I opened the Bible to read, however, I suddenly began "seeing" this film. I was clearly lucid and wide awake. I now know that what I experienced was a "vision," but never having had one before, I was clueless. In fact, no other film has ever come to me quite this way since. The only way I know how to describe it is as a series of scenes, one after another. I saw the characters; I heard the dialogue. I got out my legal pad and wrote it down as fast as it was coming to me. No longer was it a revenge tragedy; it was a comedy! *Retribution* was hysterical! As my heart was healing, and forgiveness edged out my desire to get even, a miraculous creative breakthrough occurred. I hope one day to produce this film, because it is a poignant one that speaks to many women who are left for younger women. More than that, however, the experience showed me a sliver more of the unlimited creative power God makes available to us.

It is not only in the creative, artistic arena wherein God can give divine guidance. As I've mentioned earlier, many of the world's greatest inventions and discoveries have come through dreams. Just recently I heard of a woman who had a dream showing her a particular new way of doing something,. When she acted on it, formulated a business plan, and approached a large multinational company, she walked away with a check for $200 million.

One day, during the time of rebuilding my financial life, I was on my knees asking the Lord for clients. I needed a breakthrough of some sort so that I could continue to make it. I appealed to His promises of steadfast love, daily provisions, and protection for widows. I pulled out every promise I knew in Scripture and cried out to the Lord for help. Afterwards I went to my studio to work. Within the next two hours, a creative business strategy unfolded in my mind. It was chilling to watch this business proposal become flesh. I saw it. It was brilliant and would conceivably earn my company and the company I was proposing it to over a million dollars each within the next year.

I mention these stories by way of illustration that God desires to speak to us and confirm His calling to us in many ways. I appeal to you, therefore, to keep an open mind and seek to hear Him however He chooses to speak to you.

CHAPTER 8

Determine Your Place on the
Creative Continuum

When Moses triumphantly led the Israelites out of Egypt, they were not ushered immediately into the promised land because, as the Bible explains, they were not yet ready for war. That's an important principle for us creatives to grasp. We have a tendency to think that once we've made that all-powerful commitment toward our "call," that we will somehow be rewarded for our faith. Wrong! In fact, that initial step of faith is just the first step in a serious testing phase called "adversity." The Scriptures depict it as the wilderness. I call it the "creative continuum"—that invisible line of an indeterminate number of days between the bondage and the land of promise.

I remember more than once calling my attorney during the fundraising process prior to mounting my musical and bemoaning whatever challenge I was then facing. He calmly said, "Candace, if it were easy, everybody would do it."

Pursuing our calling is the most challenging thing we will ever do. Success expert Napoleon Hill says that right after commitment almost always comes adversity, and 95% turn back at this point. It's as if there is a universal, natural Law that weeds out the weak from the strong. Proverbs hits this truth on the head, "If you faint in the day of adversity, your strength is small" (Prov. 24:10).

I wholeheartedly concur. When I made the commitment to raise the money to produce the musical, each next phase became progressively more difficult to such an extent that I sincerely doubted if I had heard the right voice. I thought, "Surely it will let up sometime." It never did. If you were to ask me, "So, why didn't you quit?" I would answer, "Because while the tests were relentless,

I kept asking for signs along the way that I was really walking the right path. The signs came." So I continued.

Emerson says,

The law of nature is growth, which often includes adversities of many kinds, yet a deep remedial force operates to turn hardship and sorrows into guides for later life, and these same hardships often serve to end some period of life which was waiting to be closed. Also, adversity breaks off certain accustomed ways of living and helps us form new ones which may be necessary for growth. The person who is tempered by hardship becomes a stronger person who can do more for himself and more for others.[8]

The Israelites had to endure the wilderness for 40 years. They would have gotten to the promised land much sooner, but that's another story, and another principle. God wasn't so much concerned with their geographical destination as He was with their heart attitude toward Him. Did they trust Him? Did they look to Him to meet their every need? Did they find their refuge in Him when times looked hopeless? Did they give thanks to Him when the good times rolled? Those were the important things to Him, and the wilderness was the only place they could learn those lessons.

On the outskirts of the promised land, Moses summarized for the people all that they had been through for the last 40 years.

You shall remember all the way which the Lord your God has led you these forty years in the wilderness, that he might humble you, testing you to know what was in your heart, whether you would keep his commandments, or not. And he humbled you and let you hunger, and fed you with manna which you did not know, nor did your fathers know; that he might make you know that man does not live by bread alone, but by everything that proceeds out of the mouth of the Lord (Deut. 8:2-3).

UNIVERSAL LAWS

There are eternal, fixed, universal laws that govern the world, and those laws are in operation regardless of a person's belief system. Galileo could have been an atheist, but nonetheless, he stumbled upon the Law of Gravity. We all know that when we drop something, it will fall to the ground. It's one of those laws that is universal. It just is.

THE LAW OF PERSONAL INITIATIVE

Many great artists, inventors, and entrepreneurs experienced adversity many times over before they arrived at success. We have to hold onto belief in our calling, belief that we are developing into what we are supposed to be, and belief that success comes only with perseverance.

Thomas Edison experienced 10,000 failures before he discovered the incandescent lamp. During that time, his house burned to the ground, and it contained all the records of his experiments. He is quoted as saying, "Well, all my failures have gone up in smoke. Now, we can start fresh." Commenting to Napoleon Hill on the eventual success of his invention, Edison said, "I finally had to succeed because I ran out of things that wouldn't work." What perseverance!

Hill says, "Adversity and defeat are turning points on the road to success. They are nature's means of refinement of men's character." Having spent 20 years researching and creating the science of success, Hill interviewed the most powerful and successful businessmen of the day: Andrew Carnegie, Franklin D. Roosevelt, John D. Rockefeller, Henry Ford, Thomas Edison, and countless more. He discovered that successful people almost invariably were successful in exact proportion to the extent to which they had met and mastered obstacles and defeat.

In the early 1800s, Samuel Morse grew up desiring to be an artist; however, it became increasingly more difficult to earn a living as one, even though he was becoming internationally known. A series of crises followed: his wife died, as did both of his parents, and Morse went to Europe to paint and reflect on his life. On the return trip aboard a ship, he was inspired by discussions at dinner about new experiments in electromagnetism and made the following comment, "If the presence of electricity can be made visible in any part of the circuit, I see no reason why intelligence may not be transmitted by electricity." Working through many difficulties and disappointments, he finally perfected and patented a new invention in 1837—what we know today as the telegraph.

Only later, after many more setbacks, did his projects receive funding. Morse, recognized today as the father of faxes, modems, e-mail, the internet and other electronic communication, once commented, "The only gleam of hope, and I cannot underrate it, is from confidence in God. When I look upward it calms any apprehension for the future, and I seem to hear a voice saying: 'If I clothe the lilies of the field, shall I not also clothe you?' Here is my strong confidence, and I will wait patiently for the direction of Providence." Remember, Samuel Morse began his destiny as an artist, a creative who had eyes to see things differently and to create something visual from nothing.

THE LAW OF THE SEASONS

There are other such laws too, such as the Law of the Seasons. God's Word says, "In everything, there is a season." That means *everything*. It is a powerful concept to meditate upon because its application is so broad. Let's say your kids are acting up and want nothing to do with you. It's seasonal. You can have hope you will have a close relationship once again. When you are bereft in grief, you will laugh again in time. When you go through illness or mental distress, hang on because it will eventually lift. When you lose a loved one, be patient because God will bring others along to help ease the hurt and stand with you through the pain.

Henry and Richard Blackaby, in their devotional book *Experiencing God*, have an insightful perspective.

The beauty in the way God designed the four seasons is that, though each one is distinct, they all work together to bring life and growth. Just as God planned seasons in na-

71

ture, he planned seasons in life as well. He has planned for times of fruitfulness and activity. He will also build in times of quiet and rest. There will be times when he asks us to remain faithful doing the same work day after day. But there will also be periods of excitement and new beginnings. By God's grace, we will enjoy seasons of harvesting the fruit of our faithfulness, and by his grace we will also overcome the cold winters of heartache and grief, for without winter there would be no spring. Just as it is with the seasons of nature, these seasons in our lives work together to bring about God's perfect will for each one of us.[9]

When I was studying about agricultural life during biblical times, it was most enlightening to discover that from God's perspective, there are really only two seasons: sowing and reaping. Yes, in our understanding, we delineate four seasons, for there are specific things that happen in the life of a seed from its planting to its full growth. Overall, however, in God's bigger picture vantage point, we are either investing time, energy, or money into our calling (sowing seeds), or we are enjoying the payoff (reaping). It's the effort and the reward, the start and the finish.

THE LAW OF THE OVERCOMERS

It is a sobering realization to see that out of the hundreds of thousands of people who began their creative continuum when the Israelites left Egypt, only a few made it! To be precise, only Joshua and Caleb and their families made it to the final destination after those 40 long years. Not even Moses made it! This fact lies behind Jesus' words that many are called, but few are chosen. In other words, only a precious few are able to withstand this testing period. I call them overcomers.

As I look at the creative seasons of my own life, I often wonder if I will be one of these overcomers. I pray so. It seems I have been in the season of the wilderness far longer than any other season. That's where I currently live on the "creative continuum." Yes, I'm further along than I was 30 years ago, further along even than I was a year ago, but I'm still there nonetheless. I believe it takes a lifetime to become truly humble enough, teachable enough, and pliable enough to be used for God's glory and not our own. We are such strong-willed creatures that our will often has to be broken (notice I said "will" and not "spirit") before we can be properly harnessed and then led in the direction we are meant to go.

My late husband, Mike, used to describe himself as an old plow mule and me as the thoroughbred—high-spirited, always pumped and ready for the race. We made quite a team. I needed his steadying gait, and at times, he needed my drive and spirit. As one who is highly charged, I have often required, I suppose, extra harnessing by the Lord. When I commit to something, I go at it 150%. Perhaps I wouldn't have to undergo so many trials if I'd just learn to slow down my pace!

Overcoming Rejection. One of my more colorful "trials" involved a screenplay I wrote called *The Audition*. It is one of my more personal stories, one that forced me to revisit many old wounds and scars from my past. The process of writing that particular story took close to three years, involved several therapy sessions, and many tears. When it was finished, I had birthed a cow. I was spent. Everything in me was on those pages, and I proudly sent it to my agent, thinking surely he would see the merit in such a character-driven, emotionally-charged story.

About a month later, I received a letter *not* from my agent, but from his assistant, wanting to "get back to me concerning my script." For three whole pages, he proceeded to tear it apart scene by scene. He may as well have split my gut open with a scalpel without benefit of anesthesia. This was at the time I was seriously contemplating moving to L.A. Suddenly I was shell-shocked. Devastated. I cried until my eyes were so swollen I could hardly see.

My 16-year old son walked into the kitchen, took one look at me and said, "What's wrong, Mom?" (pause) "Hollywood?" All I was able to muster was a quivering chin and a nod. Now, mind you, I was following the creative journey I was certain I was called to be on, and this was certainly not in the plan. *The Artist's Way* advises that when a creative goes through times like this, it helps to grieve the loss, and embrace it, if you will. So, I decided to grieve this sucker 150%!

I ran a hot bubble bath, lit a candle, closed the shower curtain, and turned on the bathroom fan (so Tyler wouldn't hear me cry). I was determined to grieve this artistic loss to the hilt. Why not? A little self-pity goes a long way sometimes.

Right in the middle of my Camille episode, Tyler knocked on the door to my bedroom. I couldn't hear him with the fan on, so told him to open the bathroom door. Picture it: he opened the door, saw the candle and the closed curtain. "Mom, you're not trying to kill yourself, are you?" Suddenly I burst into laughter and said, "Son, that would be the easy way out. I've got to live through this mess!"

For a creative, our work (our dance, our book, our audition) is an extension of our very being. So, if we experience rejection, unfortunately, we take it personally. We need to take heart, though, and realize that everyone who has gone this path before has had to endure the wilderness. It's a necessary part of the journey. Why? Because true art, one that deeply touches people, can only come from pain and solitude, where the artist's heart has been laid bare before his or her Creator.

Overcoming Temptation. I can't turn on television without stumbling upon some reality show about people wanting to be stars: *American Idol, Fame, Star Search*, and countless spinoffs. What this tells me is that in our culture, the desire for fame and personal glory is unquenchable.

God is more concerned about our relationship with Him than He is with what we do, how well we succeed, and how many people we impress. For the creative, the time may come when this question rises up in your inner voice, "Which do you want more: success or Me?"

When Jesus began His earthly ministry after being baptized by John the Baptist, His first stop was the wilderness where He was tempted by Satan. There the evil one took Jesus to a high mountain, and showed Him all the kingdoms of the world and all their glory, and said to Him, "All these I will give you, if you will fall down and worship me" (Luke 4:6).

This passage raises some serious questions, especially for the creative because the end result of earthly success in our chosen creative fields (writing, acting, singing, dancing) often brings with it fame, wealth, and glory. This passage indicates, however, that the one who has it to give is Satan. Notice Jesus did not answer back, "This is ridiculous. You don't have these things to give because they are mine." Rather, the New Testament teaches that Satan is the ruler of the earth, the "prince of the power of the air" (Ephesians 2:2).

I am not implying that everyone who has arrived at the pinnacle of success in their field has "sold out." Rather, I am saying that chances are we will each be tempted in one way or another to compromise our spiritual integrity, and we should be alert to it at all times.

Overcoming discouragement. To walk the creative journey requires choices, and those choices often carry with them serious financial consequences. When I began Quadra Entertainment, I went into hibernation for three years in order to research and write screenplays. Who paid for me to do that? No one. It was a choice I made, for it was necessary to have completed screenplays in order to pitch and establish the credibility I desired as a writer. What I did was divide my days in half. The first half of each day I devoted to my writing. That meant shutting off the phones, keeping at it every day. The rest of the time I did my ad agency work, servicing my clients' needs. However, the reality was that my income was cut in half. It was a choice I made, and the price I have paid for it.

My cousin, Dean, and I have a close relationship. The same age, we grew up together and have shared many of life's trials. One day we were discussing the different directions we each took in life. She heads up a large department in a prestigious bank, earns a handsome salary, and is building up quite a comfortable retirement package. I remarked, "Dean, maybe I took the wrong path. Look at what you've built up for yourself and your retirement future, and look at what I have." She wisely smiled and replied, "But you would have died inside doing what I do." She's right. I would have. She continued, "And I would have died doing what you do. I couldn't have stood the risk of not knowing if I were going to get a pay-check."

We often need others to remind us who we are, and that it's okay to be different. I had a momentary lapse of self-doubt. It's normal. It's human. Yes, I may reach retirement age and have nothing. But if I have followed the call I feel my Creator had for me, then I have to believe that He will care for all my needs when the time comes.

There is a balance here. It is very important for us as creatives to be wise and practical enough to cover our living expenses. We cannot be true to our art if we are stressed out by creditors. I have another friend who earns her living by providing financial counsel. Connie has been a wonderfully grounded sounding board when I have been faced with financial decisions, especially after the death of my husband. She has filled an important need in my creative life.

Every artistic person I know has had to walk this part of the journey of looking at our lives and the choices we've made, such as walking away from a good salary or a business merger, or cutting our income in half in order to venture out. The consequences of all that is at times doubt. Did I foolishly forsake financial security and a retirement pension to go out on this limb? Did I just sabotage myself? And then we go in homes where there is financial stability, wealth, abundance, and we feel we've purposely chosen the road to poverty. It's an insidious feeling, and the self-doubts can make you wonder if the whole journey has been delusional, chasing some carrot that is always illusive. If someone asked, "What do you want more: wealth or validation?" I would say the latter in a heartbeat. Because that has been my nagging doubt: "Lord, did I hear you? Was this your leading or my own convoluted ambitions?"

UNDERSTANDING THE CREATIVE JOURNEY

The creative's life is a journey, and each of its stages are important and need to be experienced fully so that we are able to encourage others along the way. Scripture is filled with story after story that illustrate the period of time we call the wilderness—the time between the call and God's confirmation.

Samuel was only a child when he first heard God's call and delivered his first message from God to the High Priest Eli. Samuel does not appear again in history for 20 years, at which time he was confirmed by the Israelites as both God's Judge and Prophet for His people, which was God's destiny or call for him. Jeremiah was likewise called by God, when he was a young boy, to be a prophet who would hear from Him and help lead His people. We know from history that 13 years later, when King Josiah needed a prophet who could tell him the mind of the Lord on a matter, he did not go to Jeremiah. Rather, he consulted a prophetess named Huldah. This tells us that Jeremiah was still somewhere on the continuum in his own personal wilderness of divine instruction. Jesus Himself was called to die for the sins of the world before the foundation of the world, and yet even He had to wait 30 years before the Father confirmed that call before the world.

Many things seem to take place during this continuum. For one, God tests our hearts to rid them of impure motives, as He did with Saul. If we don't pass the test, then either the tests become more severe or else God chooses someone else. In Saul's case, God tested him many times over many years. In each instance, Saul acted impulsively, doing his own thing rather than waiting upon God and being obedient to His commands. As a result, He chose David as King over Israel and sent Samuel to anoint him, when David was but a young man. As with Samuel and Jeremiah, David was forced to undergo 25 years of testing, adversity, and persecution before Saul died and he was confirmed King of Israel by the people. It is important to note that during those intervening 25 years, God not only tested David, but He continued to test Saul. He never ceases to desire our repentance and the turning of our hearts back to Him.

Many times we mistakenly think that the wilderness journey is just something we have to hurry through to get to the promised land, and we foolishly try to rush through it rather than stop and take honest stock of the journey. The key to God's confirmation of our personal destinies lies in the process, not so much in the destination, for it is in the process whereby we learn the skills to be what God created us to be. By the time David became King of Israel, his time in the wilderness had taught him invaluable lessons in leadership, military tactics and strategies, reading people, building leaders among his followers, and most importantly, taught him to seek the Lord and depend on Him wholly for his very survival. It was surviving the process that made him ready to realize his destiny. That's what's known as perseverance, a quality we all desperately need.

GOD'S LESSONS

Someone once said, "Your gifts will take you to a place, but your character will keep you there." Nothing purifies or stretches one's character more than the wilderness. Let me share some of the lessons I have learned that I could not have learned any place other than the wilderness.

Faith is evidenced by a major step forward into the obstacle. Faith is what pleases God. One particular day I was struggling with the myriad pressures that befall a producer and journalled about my feeling of helplessness. I have made it a habit to read at least one psalm everyday, and that day's psalm illumined a truth I hadn't seen before: "Thy way was through the sea, thy path through the great waters; yet thy footprints were unseen" (Ps. 77:19).

Once again, my attention was riveted to the story of the Israelites' journey through the wilderness. God led them to the edge of the Red Sea where they were encamped. Unbeknownst to them, Pharaoh and his entire army were closing in behind them. They were trapped and in great turmoil. They were mad at God for their circumstances, and angry with Moses for getting them in this particular predicament. But God had a most important lesson to teach not only them, but the rest of the world throughout history.

God's way is always forward. He wants us never to be in retreat, never motivated by fear and running away when it looks like we're facing a huge obstacle.

The sea was not the destination for the Israelites, it was merely an obstacle, albeit a huge obstacle. Up to this time, they had had manifestations of the Lord's very personal guidance and provision: He had been leading them by day in a pillar of cloud and at night by a pillar of fire. They should have known that He would not have led them so miraculously only to let them die by the Red Sea. But we are not always rational when we encounter obstacles like certain death.

What frustrates us is that we want a neon sign to point out the exact path. However, in His divine providence, He often covers it over. The sea did not part beforehand, so they could plainly see the path. That would have been too easy and would have required no faith. The way opened only when Moses took the first step forward, through the obstacle.

God's plan for us is on the other side of the obstacle. God clearly had a destination for them (the Promised Land), and He has one for us. Think about that: He has a unique territory in the great scheme of things with our names on it. It may be on a New York marquee, but then again, it may be directing a children's choir in our church. Whatever it is, though, it is ours, and only in that very thing will we be completely fulfilled. Our job, however, is to keep going forward and claim it when we see it.

The miracle lies within the obstacle itself. Whatever is blocking your way right now, whatever you look at and say, "There's no way I can get through this," *that* is the place of the miracle. God wants to prove His power to His people. He can't very well display it when whatever obstacle we're facing is no big deal. The Red Sea was the obstacle. It separated the Israelites from their ultimate destiny. It was either drown or be slaughtered by the Egyptians. Fortunately, God had other plans—a miracle—and in the process of their going forward, displayed His greatness and glory in a way that has sustained the faith of generations. We Christians owe a tremendous debt to our Jewish fathers of the faith for going through this journey before us to show us what a great God we have!

Just take the next step. Creatives are often future-thinkers. We play an endless mental game of what-ifs and can find ourselves bombarded with so many options that paralysis often sets in. Proverbs gives us an important principle when we become confused about which direction to take: "Let your eyes look directly forward, and your gaze be straight before you. Take heed to the path of your feet, then all your ways will be sure" (Prov. 4:25-26).

If we have reached a personal decision wherein we have declared, "Lord, I desire to follow Your leading," then we will know what to do—keep going forward on the path our feet are presently on. Believe me, God will put up a major roadblock if we are going down the wrong path. He shuts doors and opens others. What He doesn't want, though, is for us to be perplexed about our path. Just keep going. "In all your ways acknowledge him and he will make straight your paths" (Prov. 3:6). What a wonderful promise, and a great way to start each day: "Lord, lead me in the direction I'm to go today." Then get up and go to it.

I've often been called a visionary. I don't mean that to sound cocky, because what it really means is visionaries look way over there to the future and see a big picture, and we are tempted to overlook the immediacy of the path right in front of our feet. We future thinkers have to remember that we only get to the future God has for us one step at a time.

Watch your step. There is the familiar story of a man who walked down the street every day to get to work. One day there was a hole in the pavement that the man did not see. Suddenly, he fell in and arrived at work filthy, bloody, and bruised. The next day, he walked to work and once again fell into the same hole, having forgotten it was there. The third day, while walking to work, he said to himself, "Okay, I've got to watch that hole," but by the time he got to it, his mind was on the playoff game on TV that night, and sure enough, he fell once again into the hole. The fourth day, he focused with all his might not to fall into the hole. Sure enough, he got to the hole and walked around it and was proud that he made it to work in one piece. He was so proud, as a matter of fact, that he completely forgot about the hole on his way home and fell in. The fifth day, he finally decided to change tactics altogether: he walked to work on the other side of the street!

This story all too often describes the creative's journey. There are things in our paths that continue to trip us up, things that perhaps trip us up more than other people. One key reason for the journey itself is to learn to spot our own particular mine fields, covered in the next chapter, for they are placed strategically to get us off track and down into a dark hole.

CHAPTER 9

Spot *Your* Personal Mine Fields

The Scriptures teach that we have a spiritual enemy who seeks to kill, steal, and destroy (John 10:10). To accomplish his goal, he deploys surreptitious tactics or mine fields designed to derail our individual paths. I have come to realize that the more noble our calling, the more mines are thrown into our path to destroy us. Take heart, then, if you have found the journey difficult, for most likely, yours is a truly noble calling. Take heart, too, for the steadfast love of the Lord is your comfort.

The apostle Paul describes this unseen battlefield.

> *We are not contending against flesh and blood, but against the principalities, against the powers, against the world rulers of this present darkness, against the spiritual hosts of wickedness in the heavenly places. Therefore take the whole armor of God that you may be able to withstand in the evil day* (Eph. 6:12-13).

It isn't true that only Jesus, the apostles and well-known teachers and preachers are targets for demonic attacks. The enemy's target is every person who has made a decision to walk with God and follow His commandments. Look at the first chapter of Job. Job was a target only because he was a good man.

Jesus exercised complete authority over every demon He encountered throughout His earthly ministry and gives us this same authority. He said, "I have given you authority to tread upon serpents and scorpions, and over all the power of the enemy; and nothing shall hurt you" (Luke 10:18). The problem is, we often are too dense to recognize that whatever is holding us back could actually be demonic. Furthermore, we fail to do battle with the enemy in the authority God gives us.

Paul said, "Though we live in the world, we are not carrying on a worldly war, for the weapons of our warfare are not worldly but have divine power to destroy strongholds" (2 Cor. 10:3-4). Those of us who call ourselves Christians, in whom the Spirit of Christ dwells, fail many times to exercise the authority we do have.

Throughout the production of the musical, *A Time To Dance*, I experienced the reality of the spiritual battlefield. I have known demonic attacks many times in my life before, and clearly recognized them. The spiritual message the musical conveyed was being threatened: illness of the star, rancor between key crew members, jealousy and delusional outbursts, along with unbelievable financial challenges. Many times my associate producer and I had to pull aside and pray together, binding the evil forces that were trying to destroy what God wanted to accomplish through the musical.

I recall a very unusual encounter following the premiere. I was in our Atlanta production office, wrapping up myriad production and financial details, when an acquaintance made an appointment to see me. I actually thought it was to be a business meeting until she said, "I'm not here to discuss business today. On the way over, God told me you have been under severe satanic attack, and I'm here to pray for you and encourage you." I was floored. I hardly knew this woman, and yet here she was telling me, "The enemy is trying to destroy the work you are doing." What she didn't know was that for the past four days the Lord had been revealing the same thing to me: that I was up against a major stronghold and needed to know how to do battle better.

When I know I am under attack, some of the things I have learned to do are:

1- Ask my friends for prayer. Nothing defeats the enemy's power more than prayer.

2- Praise the Lord's goodness out loud. The enemy cannot be in the presence of someone who is praising the Lord. Thus, when negative thoughts and doubts try to engage my mind, I have to take action and refuse to listen to the voices and speak out loud the promises of God and His goodness.

In the weeks that followed the premiere (the toughest test of all, discussed in Chapter 11), what got me through was turning my creative energies into writing a song of praise. I spent hours and days on this song, and the oppression finally lifted.

There are many fine books on the market concerning spiritual warfare. I recommend study in this area if you are unfamiliar with how to do battle in a spiritual sense, and most especially, if you sense this area has been a stumbling block for you.

There are undoubtedly many more, but at this writing I have uncovered seven minefields and more than 30 individual mines to which creatives are particularly vulnerable. Webster defines "mines" as something intentionally placed underground to cause the collapse of an enemy. By learning to spot those that we stumble upon most often, we will learn to shore up our defenses, avoid them altogether, and ultimately extend our chances to reach our final destinations. I encourage you to take special note, and even circle, those that tend to derail you. (Note: I comment more on the ones that have derailed me for a season.)

MINEFIELD #1
INTERNAL WEAKNESSES

This particular mine field is such a killer because it is lodged in our minds, our greatest battleground. That's why Scripture continues to exhort us to "not be conformed to this world, but be transformed by the renewal of our minds" (Rom. 12:2). The Apostle Paul says, "For though we live in the world we are not carrying on a worldly war, for the weapons of our warfare are not worldly but have divine power to destroy strongholds" (2 Cor. 10:3-4) .These strongholds are mental. They are powerful mental constructs and belief systems that usually have been with us a long time. Notice in Paul's words, however, that the power of the Holy Spirit will destroy them. First, though, we have to recognize them.

FEAR. When the Israelites were up against the Red Sea on one side and the Egyptian army barreling down behind them, they were terrified. There is great application in the creative's life because the emotion we battle most in walking through our wilderness is fear.

We would rather stop and encamp by the sea and tremble for the rest of our lives rather than follow the only recourse given to us and go forward. God never wants us to bow the knee to fear. Rather, He wants us to be strengthened in our spirit, knowing that He promised never to leave us or forsake us. He wants us to walk forward in faith.

My late husband was a wonderful man, but he was oppressed by fear. Having been severely scarred by Viet Nam, a broken marriage, a horrific custody battle, and finally the shattered dream of his own homebuilding company, he had allowed a stronghold of fear to take root. He wasn't knowledgeable in how to remove the stronghold, and became so convinced that if he stepped out again something worse would happen, he simply chose to stop. Even though I knew he loved me very much, life itself was too difficult. Unable to battle the continual mental onslaught of the enemy, he gave up and wanted to die. Mike's death was sudden, without warning. There was no pain, he simply took his last breath. Personally, I don't believe God took him out of any form of punishment. Rather, I believe our loving heavenly Father knew Mike didn't have the heart to go on and beckoned, "Come on home, son." I miss him, for he was a gifted, creative man for whom the wilderness was extremely difficult.

FEELINGS OF INADEQUACY. Remember when God called Moses to go back to Egypt and free His people, the first words out of his mouth was, "Who am I that I should go?" I don't believe God ever calls us to do something for which we feel capable, where we think, "It's about time You asked me to do that. I know exactly how to get the job done." If that were our response, the journey would be taken without faith, in our own strength. There is no glory for God in that. Rather, God chooses "what is foolish in the world to shame the wise...what is weak in the world to shame the strong... so that no human being might boast in the presence of God" (1 Cor. 1:27-29).

One night I was watching the Tony Awards the year following the premiere of my musical. I was amazed at the musical and choreographing genius of that year's nominees. The more I watched, the more inadequate I felt. Who was I to think myself capable of writing a quality musical? I went to bed totally disheartened. During the night, I had a very significant dream. In the dream, I was emptying my shopping cart at the grocery check-out stand, but seemingly there was another one belonging to a friend. I stared into the other cart and noticed it contained fancy Italian bread along with various kinds of imported peppers and sausages. Looking over at my cart, the contents were boring and bland. I woke up. Again, it was one of those dreams wherein I had the sense God wanted to say something to me. What He said to me was this: "My child, I have given you everything you need in your grocery cart to create something that will be life-sustaining. It may not be fancy imported peppers or freshly-baked bread, but what I want you to do is to correct the tendency of yours to look in the other person's cart rather than in your own. Be grateful for what you have been given. Give thanks for those things, and leave the results to Me."

ENVY AND RESENTMENT. One of the most surefire ways to derail is when we harbor negative feelings over the success of others. Creatives are typically driven and ambitious, walk a lonely path, and are terribly insecure. One of our chief motivations (remember the motivational patterns) is hearing and seeing the praise of others. We live for the applause, the reviews, the project sale, and the deal. That motivation can become so strong that we resent when others are given their moment in the sun. In the creative arts, the competition is stiff. There is always someone else grabbing for the part, or the limelight, or top billing. It is not easy to develop true friends in the industry because there seem to be so many knives aimed at our backs.

There is a powerful warning in Proverbs: "Do not rejoice when your enemy falls, and let not your heart be glad when he stumbles; lest the Lord see it, and be displeased, and turn away his anger from him" (Prov. 24:17-18). In other words, if we envy others' success—even if we *do* deserve it more than they—God says He will give it to them because our motives are wrong! We must realize that we are each on our own journeys, and God is ultimately concerned about our getting there with pure hearts. There have been many times when I've had to silently bow my head and confess these feelings. Our divine call is not to success. Our call is to holiness to such an extent that God would rather see us off the journey completely rather than to arrive with an impure heart.

LAZINESS. This is a tough one for me to describe. I may be many things, but I am not lazy. However, I do know brilliantly creative people who spend their creative energy in some mental fantasy rather than putting their hand to the plow. Scripture is very clear about laziness. "Love not sleep, lest you come to poverty; open your eyes, and you will have plenty of bread" (Prov. 20:13) and "A little sleep, a little slumber, a little folding of the hands to rest, and poverty will come upon you like a robber, and want like an armed man" (Prov. 24:33-34). I would imagine that the only anecdote for laziness is to seek out an accountability partner who will hold your feet to the fire, to help cheer you on a clearly formulated action plan for achieving small steps at a time.

DISCOURAGEMENT. This can be a killer. "Hope deferred makes the heart sick" (Prov. 13:12). I know that verse by heart. I have prayed it back to God many times, reminding Him, "Lord, You don't want my heart to get sick, so please get me out of this discouragement!" I would recommend both a practical and a spiritual counter to times of discouragement. Practically speaking, wait it out. If I am going through a particularly bad time and have a project proposal to make, or if I'm pitching a business deal, I wait until it is a better time to experience the rejection if it comes. I have learned to read my moods. After *A Time To Dance* crumbled in my face, the wind was knocked out of me. I had absolutely no heart to receive any other rejection or disappointment. Thus, while in that emotional state, I withheld putting myself in any of those situations wherein I could be rejected. I placed myself in a protective bubble and showed up daily before the Lord waiting for His healing balm to soothe the deeper places. The danger, of course, is that we can feel so safe in that bubble, we may never venture forth again. But if that drive and call rises up inside our bellies to get back out there in the wilderness, we will be miserable staying in the bubble. We will know it's time and venture forth again.

King David was often discouraged. His method of dealing with it was to pour out all his feelings to the Lord. There is no shame in feeling discouraged. The shame is in using our tongues only to speak of our discouragement and never the declarations of faith. David says, "Why are you cast down, O my soul..." (i.e., "why are you discouraged, self?") "Hope in God; for I shall again praise him, my help and my God" (Ps. 42:5). The spiritual answer to discouragement is a declaration of our faith in the Lord. Many times over the past two years, the only thing that has gotten me through has been making declarations: "Lord, I refuse to look at my present circumstances. I choose to believe and declare that You are my refuge and my strength, my present help in time of trouble. You are my cup and my portion, my protector, my rock, and my shield. I look to You to fight this battle for me."

GUILT. The one thing the Lord requires of us is to have an open heart before Him by starting each day with words such as, "Search me, O God, and know my thoughts...See if there be any wicked way in me" (Ps. 139:23-24). Waiting before the Lord after a prayer such as this is just that: being quiet before Him. He will reveal those things that need confessing. I have been derailed from my journey several times in my life because I failed to allow His scrutinizing light to shine on me and pinpoint my sinfulness.

Following my divorce, I was left with a residue of bitterness and anger against many people. I felt justified in holding onto them. I remember the time I went back to the church to which my ex-husband had originally been called as the pastor. Several people within that church had caused hurt and pain to both Tom and me, and following the divorce, I found myself blaming them that my marriage had fallen apart. Miserably I sat in the pew farthest in the back. There was no way I could worship with those negative feelings clogging up my heart. I was about to be blown apart by the landmine known as guilt. God was dealing with me sharply.

I had a critical choice: keep on harboring the hateful feelings (and derail myself completely from my destiny), or admit them, seek forgiveness, and keep on the journey. God was teaching me an important truth: "Let Me worry about what they did wrong. You are only responsible before Me for your wrong. Should you be harboring this bitterness in your heart?" Ouch. There is only one way out around guilt. It is one of the more difficult things we are ever asked to do, and yet God demands a pure heart if we are to keep on with the journey to our destiny. "See to it that no one fail to obtain the grace of God; that no root of bitterness spring up and cause trouble, and by it the many become defiled" (Heb. 12:15).

One at a time, I made appointments with the three men with whom I had become embittered. Tearfully, I admitted I had been torn up with anger toward them and asked them to forgive me. The Lord had prepared all of them for my coming. They graciously received me and confessed their own parts in contributing to my hurt. There was tremendous reconciliation and unbelievable peace.

NEGATIVE THINKING PATTERNS. I make it a practice to surround myself only with friends who possess positive thinking patterns. We need all the encouragement we can get on the journey of life, and nothing saps us any more than negative thinkers. Since this "mine" is in the internal weakness category, rather than in the "wrong people in your life" mine field, I will address it this way: By surrounding ourselves with positive friends, we protect ourselves against this particular "mine." Negative friends mirror to us the negative thinking to which we can all sometimes fall prey.

I have given those closest to me permission to alert me when I get off base. It is so critical to be accountable to someone who is as committed to my successful completion of the journey as I am to theirs. The best friends are ones who know when to just listen while you get discouragement and confusion out of your system and know when to say, "Okay, that's enough. You've got to get a grip now and move forward."

One particularly dangerous negative thinking pattern is the Poverty Mentality where we conclude that God only has hardship and poverty for His children. The opposite can be just as deadly: Prosperity Thinking, which asserts that God's blessings only come with a Mercedes or Jaguar decal on them. Both are destructive patterns.

Proverbs 28:19 is a wonderful promise: "He who tills his land will have plenty of bread, but he who follows worthless pursuits will have plenty of poverty." The truth is that when we really plow our creative soil, work it, root out the weeds, nourish it with Truth, watch over it and protect it from predators, and learn how to produce the right crops for the soil, when our energy is poured out faithfully day after day in this effort, we have a divine promise that we will have plenty of bread! Mind you, it may not be caviar, but it will be plenty of what God provides to sustain us!

As an aside, I want to note that some plots of ground are harder to till than others. A gold mine is much harder to extract fruit from than a barley field. Thus, for some whose destiny is connected with mining for gold or diamonds, where the ground requires picks and axes, it is reasonable to assume that the time until pay-off is much greater.

UNCLEAR GOALS AND LACK OF ACTION PLAN. I lumped these two mines together because they go hand in hand, as a kind of a double-whammy explosion. It is very easy for creatives to be vague when it comes to clarifying their main desire, or "naming their seed." Likewise, if we don't clarify what it is we truly want, based on who we were created to be, then we will get derailed from this "mine" and be unable to articulate a realistic, workable action plan.

I was fortunate in the mid-90s to meet a woman who became a mentor and business coach. I fought contracting with a coach because as a Christian, it seemed like a cop-out to look to someone other than the Lord for clarification and direction. I have since learned, however, that God gifts other personality types in such a way as to be of tremendous value to creatives. Mariette, with my encouragement I humbly admit, has begun to focus her coaching business almost exclusively on creatives, for she sees the value that her critical thinking skills bring to them. In fact, she guides the careers of creatives all over the country, and the successes of their careers attest to her abilities as a coach.

As a conceptualizer, ideas are always coming to me. I am forever analyzing some strategy I've just conceived, working on a new project, or laying out business projections for yet another entity. Mariette has the ability to listen to all of the detailed minutiae and say, "Oh, what you're doing is ____!" And she undoubtedly has a word for it. She has summed up 15 minutes of creative effusing and crystallized them into a 5-second sound bite. Stunned, I am endlessly chagrined that she has pinpointed my dilemma so easily, and then helps me outline very clear, measurable, attainable goals. I have learned much from her and highly recommend having a coach.

PRIDE AND ENTITLEMENT. This is an area in which all gifted creatives battle. If we are gifted in something—and especially if that giftedness carries with it a divine anointing—people are going to be moved or touched by it. The tendency is then for them to heap praise and glory onto us. When that happens, we play those compliments over and over in our minds, don't we? Oh how we love to hear the praise! The Scriptures are very clear how God feels about pride: "Pride goes before destruction, and a haughty spirit before a fall" (Prov. 16:18). "The haughty looks of man shall be brought low, and the pride of men shall be humbled; and the Lord alone will be exalted in that day" (Is. 2:11).

Why does God hate pride so much? It is because this was the mine that blew Lucifer out of his place in the heavens. "How you are fallen from heaven, O Day Star, son of Dawn! How you are cut down to the ground, you who laid the nations low! You said in your heart, 'I will ascend to heaven; above the stars of God I will set my throne on high...I will make myself like the Most High'" (Isaiah 14:12-14).

Lucifer was the most beautiful, gifted creature Almighty God created. LaMar Boschman, in his enlightening book, *The Rebirth of Music*, explains that long before God made man or even formed the earth, He created three archangels: Michael, Gabriel, and Lucifer. These three had the unspeakable privilege of being closer to the throne of God than all the other celestial beings. Lucifer was uniquely different from the other two: he was the music angel. According to Ezekiel, Lucifer had timbrels and pipes built into his body. He excelled in the ability to play these instruments because they were actually part of him. Boshman writes, "Lucifer's makeup represented most categories of musical instruments that we have today: string, wind, and percussion. Not only was Lucifer a musician, but he was also the instrument as well. He was given a definite anointing for serving or ministering in music."[10]

Pride was the "mine" that destroyed Lucifer. Almighty God does not want us to be likewise derailed from our destiny. I can't help but think of so many brilliant musicians who have openly sold out to Lucifer. They even sing about him and offer him praise and thanksgiving. After all, he imbued them with fame and wealth, and he gets the glory. It shouldn't surprise us why there is so much media hype over the glamour of being a music star, and why so many young people long to be one too. Who, ultimately, is glorified, and who will demand their obedience in exchange for giving them fame?

God hates pride so much that He will do anything and everything to sensitize His children to it. I remember sitting in an entertainment industry meeting where the "in" thing was to create all this hype around yourself and declare how hot your stuff was. I shuttered inside hearing my friends cheer on each other's braggadocio comments with, "That's right...you go, girl!" My friend jabbed me in the side and whispered, "Just tell them what all you've done with *A Time To Dance*." I thought to myself, "Not on your life!" I know what God does when we become proud!

Early in my music career, I had a one-woman show performing the college circuit. This was in the days of Carole King and Carly Simon, two women singer/songwriters whose talents I admire tremendously. It wasn't long before I thought I was hot stuff. I had gained a following, and praises and accolades were abundant. Suddenly, one day, something unspeakable happened: I forgot my opening song! Mind you, I did not have a band that could keep on playing while I tried to recover the lyrics. I was it! There I was playing the piano, with sounds like a cow giving birth coming out of my mouth. This had never happened to me before, and I wasn't "cool" about forgetting lyrics at all. I should have stopped, tried to make a joke, and gone on to the next song. But I didn't. I kept on, and while these unintelligible moans poured out of my mouth, watched audience members look at each other like, "What is she doing? This is awful!" How I continued with the program is beyond me, but I did. What proceeded to happen next was that for many years, I suffered unbearable stagefright and was terrified I would forget my opening number, which inevitably I did.

Since then, I have become extremely sensitive to watching out for this particular "mine." I know all too well that the Lord has His ways of humbling us, even before a prideful thought crosses the mind. I recently heard a famous writer and speaker say that he had experienced times where he would freeze before an audience and not be able to say anything, for ten or fifteen minutes. Suddenly, he would "come to" and be as baffled as his listeners. Other times, he would stammer uncontrollably or lose his train of thought. Another time, he fell off the podium altogether. The apostle Paul was even given a thorn in his flesh to keep him from being proud about his revelatory giftedness and experiences. Yes, the Lord is extremely creative with the ways He triggers this particular mine in our lives before it blows us out of the game completely! I once heard a wise speaker say that God longs to give great giftedness to His children, but finds so few who are able to handle the glory and attention that come with it.

DEPRESSION. I want to be very careful how I address this particular "mine." I have seen friends totally crippled in life by depression, and I don't want to minimize its devastation. However, I have to be honest. I am frankly concerned that we too easily turn to medication before honestly seeking the Lord for the root cause.

In an earlier chapter, I made the statement that depression is one of the creative's clear signposts that something is amiss in his life. I truly believe this. I went through a six-month depression, which forced me into self-examination and seeking the Lord for answers. Had I turned to an antidepressant, I doubt I would ever have experienced the liberation that came from the enlightenment I eventually received.

Creative people by nature—and I certainly can attest to this—tend to be a little "manic depressive." I don't mean classifiable, necessarily, but we easily experience creative highs as well as deep melancholia. That's why others call it the artistic temperament. We're just not black and white, gut-it-out, grab-it-and-growl type people.

I remember one year I pushed myself to complete two screenplays. The work schedule was grueling, for with each screenplay comes months of researching, character delineating complete with bios and back stories, outlining, and then writing the story in proper screenplay format. Of course during those times, I earned no money for this work, and thus had to devote the other half of my days to my ad agency to put food on the table. By the time I completed the second screenplay, I was physically and emotionally spent. I should have been: I had given birth to two "children" in the time it should have taken to birth only one! During the weeks that followed, I was listless, had no energy or drive, and wasn't particularly happy when I woke up in the morning—all of which are totally foreign to my normal make-up. One day, I was talking to a good friend who knows me very well, and she insightfully remarked, "You know what? You're depressed." It was an illuminating realization because I had never before understood what depression actually felt like. It was a deep core of hopelessness. The light was out at the end of a very long tunnel.

Responsible person that I am, I went to my doctor, who promptly put me on antidepressants. Within two days I was so wired, I thought my brain would pop. I tried another brand and was equally as wired. I concluded, "forget this!" and took myself off of them. Weeks went by and soon the energy began to be restored, ever so slowly. I then realized that if we physically have post-partum depression after childbirth, it only makes sense that we would have it after birthing creative children as well. I believe we have to be patient, not get under the pile, and let nature take its course.

BUSYNESS AND PROCRASTINATION. These two go hand in hand because they deal with the misuse of time, although in different extremes. There is an obsessive-compulsion within our culture that is anathema to what our creative souls truly need. At times we need to be still, reflective, spiritually quiet, and meditative. For many people, these things are foreign. Busyness can become a convenient excuse for why we aren't further along on our particular journey. We need to take honest stock of ourselves to see if we are merely using this as a scapegoat for a deeper reason: that we are afraid to take the leap and really commit to our calling for fear we will fail. It is far easier to hide behind these two mines.

INTROSPECTION. This mine is a favorite among us introverts because we love nothing more than to sort out, analyze, edit, and sift through our thoughts and feelings. If you think about it, this analytical ability is the very key to certain creative abilities. The danger lies, however, in our giving way to it and turning the gift inward, onto ourselves. Leanne Payne's book, *The Healing Presence,* devotes an entire chapter to introspection. She writes, "To be is to experience life firsthand, to live in the present moment. The person who has the disease of introspection, who thinks painfully, constantly, and in circles about life, lives always in the painful past and for the future. In this way, he squanders his present by trying to figure out a more secure or less painful future. The future, of course, never arrives, for it is in the present moment that we 'live and move and have our being.'"[11] Ms. Payne describes famous writer C.S. Lewis' battle with introspection. Once Lewis recognized introspection as a sin and forsook it, his creativity never stopped growing and expanding.

The attractiveness of this mine has to do many times with the very nature of who creatives are: we are a people who long to find meaning and purpose in life and are also prone to thinking in the future. John Sandford, gifted teacher, writer, and counselor, says it's as if we see the final scene completely, but then have no idea how to comprehend the process of getting there. What happens along the way, then, is we try to "figure it all out." The only thing that I have found helpful in releasing me from this mine's grip is to "bring my thoughts captive to the obedience of Christ" (2 Cor. 10:5), refuse to think about them any more, and purposely choose to get outside myself and give my energy to someone else's needs.

NOT GIVING OUT TO OTHERS. This mine relates strongly to the previous one. It is easy for creatives to be so concerned about our own creative journey—what we need to do to achieve or what skill we need to perfect to get ahead—that our gifts begin to dry up completely. We become like the Dead Sea where water comes in, but doesn't flow outward, and we lose the ability to provide new life and refreshment to others, which is the reason the gifts were given to us to begin with.

In trying to rebuild my financial life following 9-11, I met a dear couple who have since become close friends. They were likewise going through a period of financial testing and were trying to formulate plans to secure new construction business. Talking with them one day, it became obvious that what they needed was business presentation materials, which is what I do for a living. I wrestled with myself for days, reasoning, *I can't do this for them for free! I know how much time it takes to design a logo, write, and produce a brochure, and on and on. After all, I'm trying to rebuild my financial life. I can't take time away from that to help these people.*

That was not a good response. I had the very gifts they needed to get ahead. The Lord may as well have been sitting right next to me, I heard His convicting words clearly: "Your gifts were given to help others." Early one morning, I called these friends and proposed a barter: "If you will wallpaper my two bathrooms, I will design your logo and produce your brochure." They jumped at the chance. They had gifts and talents I needed, and I used mine to help them. Together, with the right attitudes back in place, we were all able to move forward on our journeys.

There are countless other mines lying unseen in our internal minefield. Others that have been brought to my attention are: LACK OF FAITH, LACK OF DISCIPLINE, SELF-CONDEMNATION, and ADDICTIONS (to alcohol, drugs, prescription medication, sex, etc.) Once again, I encourage you to examine the internal ones that lure you off your path. Only when we locate them and stare them down are we then able to avoid them and even more important, diffuse them.

MINE FIELD #2:
EXTERNAL CIRCUMSTANCES

Frankly, there are some circumstances that we are helpless to resolve. I list them nonetheless, for if you see your primary mine field here, I would encourage you to seek prayer, support, and counsel from others who can help bear your burden while you are going through this part of the wilderness.

FINANCIAL SITUATION. As I've mentioned before, creatives tend to be right-brained people. We don't operate with a ledger sheet or a profit/loss statement imprinted inside our eyelids. We also tend to be very idealistic and childlike, ever sure we are to do what we are doing, oblivious to ever-dwindling funds and without realistic plans for earning more. I have a dear friend who is one of the most gifted musicians I know. Time and again, however, his creatively-geared work choices put his family in financial jeopardy. The marriage is strained because of it.

In my own case, after Mike's death, I purposely sought to surround myself with friends who could be a "voice of reason" to balance my sometimes "pie-in-the-sky" thinking. It is no sin to be inclined toward a strong right-brain. The sin is in the failure to call out for left-brained help and accountability in these matters. I highly recommend Crown Financial Ministries, accessible on-line at www.crown.org. Crown offers counseling by phone and a vast resource library for guiding creatives down a wise financial path.

FAMILY TURMOIL. If a person finds himself in a bad marriage, or one with constant upheaval, it is likely he will get stuck on the journey until those obstacles work themselves out. I know a woman who is gifted, and ambitious, yet her reality is that she has five children under the age of eleven. This could be the most well-behaved group of children in the world, and yet I would safely say that God will most likely postpone her creative "arrival" until after she has been faithful to meet her present responsibilities as a mother.

My son knows I am a workaholic. I have been guilty many times of putting my projects, my deadlines, or my creative brainstorms ahead of him. When Mike and I married, we were in a blended family situation, which was extremely difficult. I no longer had the peace and quiet to which I had become accustomed, and which I knew I needed to create. Creatively, my career stalled. During the stall, however, the Lord had a lot of dealing to do with my unwillingness to give myself to my family rather than to my projects. After all, creative children don't talk back, aren't rude, and are always appreciative of the attention we give them. It's no wonder we tend to think our real calling is to some anonymous and impersonal crowd of people rather than to our own family members, who might be hard to deal with at times.

HEALTH ISSUES. Frankly, there are times in the wilderness when we are physically sidelined. I have found that in my own life, the Lord has desired to deal with an internal healing as well as a physical one. Following my divorce, I developed some alarming symptoms: I would occasionally become numb on the left side of my body. One particular day, I needed to drive my son Tyler to a soccer game just as one of these attacks hit. I called my doctor's office and spoke to the nurse who said she would consult the doctor and call me back. Driving to the soccer game with my six-year-old in the car, the phone rang. The nurse said, "The doctor says you need to come right over to the emergency room to be checked out." You can guess what happened next. My head started throbbing, and I became convinced I was going to have a stroke right then and crash the car with my son in it. I became absolutely distraught, but of course pretended to Tyler as if everything was fine. The throbbing became worse, and I pulled off the side of the road to call for help.

Since Mike and I were already dating at the time, he came and got Tyler and took me onto the hospital. I lay in bed for two of the longest days in my life, wired to heart monitors to anticipate any potential trouble. Fortunately, I was not having a stroke, and I was soon released. However, I plunged into months of battle with anxiety and panic attacks. Throughout this painful sideline in my life, the Lord uncovered a deep-seated problem: I was carrying around the weight of the world on my shoulders, rather than following Peter's exhortation to "cast all your cares on him, for he cares about you" (1 Pet. 5:7).

One particular day while meditating on that verse, I took out my yellow legal pad and asked the Lord to show me what I was carrying around on my shoulders and assuming responsibility for controlling. I was shocked to fill up three legal pages, front and back so quickly. No wonder I almost short-circuited! What followed then was a casting ceremony wherein I literally "cast" my cares onto the Lord in my own way: inside a file folder tucked away in a cabinet in my office. There the list was dated and "cast," and whenever I was tempted to take up each of those responsibilities and concerns again, I would go back to the file, pull out the sheet and say, "No, I'm not going to worry about that. It belongs to the Lord now." I have had many such casting ceremonies.

DISTRACTIONS. I have a good friend who is extremely gifted in the film industry. Her heart's desire is to be a successful film and television producer, and she is highly regarded by many. One of the mines she struggles with most is distractions: people calling her endlessly, trying to set up appointments with her to such an extent that she lives in a frenzy most of the time, never feeling she has accomplished what she is meant to do. The only recourse against this foe—also known as the "tyranny of the urgent"—is an inner resolve and definitive follow through. It is the choice of one motivation (to complete a task) over another (to be sought after). When I am writing a project, such as this book, I tell those closest to me that my phone will be shut off during such and such period of time. If I don't, I will get sidetracked by distractions as well. This is the only way that works for me.

MINE FIELD #3: BITTER ROOTS

I dealt with this subject in Chapter 5 and cannot stress enough the importance of attending to deep-seated unresolved issues. Whatever we need to do—therapy, support groups, reading, prayer, go to others to confess—deal with it. The Scriptures are very clear about what happens when we harbor something against others. In the Sermon on the Mount, Jesus said, "If you are offering your gift [i.e., creative talents] at the altar, and there remember that your brother has something against you, leave your gift there before the altar and go; first be reconciled to your brother, and then come and offer your gift." (Matt. 5:23-24) If the first step on the journey is to consecrate our gifts and talents to God as our act of worship, then Jesus is saying that we can't even do that until we make peace. There are always people who treat us wrongly. As much as possible, however, God's way is through peace. He exhorts us to pray for our enemies and for those who persecute us. That's His way and the only way to reach the final destination.

MINE FIELD #4
WRONG PEOPLE IN OUR LIVES

KEEPERS OF THE GATE. These are the people whom we empower to call the shots in directing our lives. Why we have them I'll never know, and I cannot possibly tell you how sick and tired I am of the ones I have allowed into my life. One thing I know, though, is how to recognize them.

My first gatekeeper was a script consultant I hired as a fledgling screenwriter. She had come highly recommended by people in the industry and seemed to have the inside scoop on navigating through the Hollywood maze. That was attractive to me. So I hired her to read my first script (into which I had poured five years of my life) and give me feedback. Her *modus operandi* was that if she liked a script, she would open the doors to producers she knew who were looking for good stories to produce. What a shtick! For someone from Georgia, this was the holy grail! Someone with an "in" to Hollywood! I could hardly wait for her phone call, fully expecting to hear, "This is the most marvelous story I've ever read." I suppose all writers have an ego the size of Texas. Otherwise, we would never venture forth to write. For the next hour, however, she dissected my script like a lab exercise in advanced biology. I felt fileted. When I hung up the phone, I thought that I must not have one iota of talent. *The Artist's Way* calls this experience "shaming criticism." I didn't know its name then. I was new in the game. This woman is a perfect example of a "keeper of the gate." If I made it past her, then I would gain Hollywood acceptance. If I didn't, then I was blocked from going forward in my writing goals.

After an eternity in a fetal position, I finally ventured forth to get a grip and see what I could learn from this experience, knowing that even the worst experiences teach us something. I re-wrote the script, utilizing many of her suggestions, and clearly, it is now a much better script. But because it was a big-budget film, I knew I would not easily place the script with a studio because I was still an unknown. I changed tactics. I called her back and said I was getting ready to work on my next screenplay—a low-budget one—and wanted her input on which idea to pursue. She said, "Great." I proceeded to describe some five projects in my ideas file. Which one did she believe was most marketable? She picked my favorite. Bingo. I had her. For sure she was going to love this screenplay because it was made to order for my keeper of the gate! After a year and a half of research and completion of the screenplay, I booked a phone consult with her, and once again paid for her critique. I could hardly wait for the appointed phone call. I couldn't wait to hear her elation over a project she had a part in birthing. A pity creatives can't control their fantasy life!

The call came and the first words out of her mouth were, "I

know you want to hear blah, blah, blah....buttttt." I tuned out after that. I don't know when I had ever felt so crushed. Did nobody get what I wrote? Or was I a horrible writer? You can imagine which I concluded. It took months for me to venture forth again. I had lost so much confidence in my abilities, I contemplated giving up writing altogether.

After much thought, I decided to try Hollywood one more time, this time with a different consultant. I sent her that second script and held my breath until our scheduled one-hour phone consult. I paced the floors in anticipation. From the first few minutes of our conversation, she affirmed me as a writer, encouraged the lines of thought I was reasoning through the plotline, and understood the character twists I was crafting along the way. The consult was liberating. *Finally*, I thought, *someone who understands how my mind works, and actually champions it!* The suggestions that she made were helpful and insightful, such as, "I understand what you're trying to do here, and if you feel that strongly about saying it that way, then I encourage you to follow your instincts." When she offered constructive criticism, her suggestions were insightful and didn't make me feel ashamed that I didn't do it right. I will always be grateful for her affirmation, and the many things she taught me.

What I learned from these experiences has become very valuable. Creatives often come into contact with those "wanna be's" who didn't, so they became critics or teachers. To a student's eyes or a younger artist, they appear all-wise and all-knowing, and we foolishly grant power to them to approve or negate our art. These are the "keepers of the gate," and believe me, they are our enemies! They are the enemies to every creative who ever dared to speak out, to dance the great dance, to sing their guts out, or to paint as if there were no canvas left.

Another lesson I have learned is that as we mature on our creative journey, we reach (or should reach) the time where we begin to affirm and empower ourselves. When I reached this stage, it became a major turning point. I no longer looked to others to "make it happen for me." I began to trust in *my* leading, along with the talents God had entrusted *me* with. That doesn't mean I close myself off to constructive criticism. This is where discernment comes in: we have to be able to tell the difference between sincere helpers and the destructive keepers of the gate. How do we do that? It's simple. When someone gives you his "opinion" or "helpful criticism" about your art, how do you feel? Do you feel illumined, like, "A-ha...I see what he means! Yes, that makes sense!" Or, do you somehow feel shamed? If you feel the latter, stay away from that person like the plague.

Napoleon Hill's philosophy is, "With every adversity comes the seed of equivalent benefit." Julia Cameron says it this way: "Every artistic loss must always be viewed as a potential gain. It's all in the framing." I could have concluded that I simply wasn't good enough as a writer to do what I wanted to do. Or, I could see it an entirely new way: that I was being taught the importance of self-affirmation and instructed in taking back the creative controls of my life. Had I continued to defer my power to others, I would ultimately have missed the thrill of producing my own work and seeing it touch audiences the way it did.

Two others in this category that bear mentioning are fairly self-explanatory: TEMPTERS, those who lure us away from what we know our path to be, and PARASITES, those who hang onto us hoping that through us they can achieve their goals through osmosis rather than looking to the Lord for His direction, or looking within themselves to hone their skills and walk their own journey. Allow me to go into a little more detail on two additional mines in this mine field that bear further commentary.

CRITICAL FAMILY/FRIENDS. Almost every creative has those within his closest family circle who are not supportive of his creative journey. If truth be known, these people may wrestle with all sorts of inner motivations: They may be jealous of our gifts or want us to walk the same dull, unappealing lives they chose. If we succeed, then how will they feel knowing they could have made the effort to achieve that same thing? We will never know what truly lurks behind comments such as, "I think you're being unrealistic...get a real job and get your head out of the clouds."

As life proceeds, the creative fork takes a much sharper angle than the path chosen by the majority of the pack. At this juncture, the creative truly feels like an outcast. I cannot stress enough the importance of limiting association with those negative influences in our lives and shoring ourselves up with those who understand, accept, and champion us. It is especially difficult if one of the critical friends turns out to be a spouse. In such a case, God would certainly not advocate divorce. Rather, the wisdom would seem to be this: balance that negative perspective with other positive people.

Once my decision was made to begin my entertainment development company, I hibernated for three years in order to write. Mike was supportive of my creative pursuits but was frankly leery of my associating with too much "Hollywood." He feared I would turn away from our life together by the lure of the carrot known as Fame. These were fears and insecurities that he had to deal with. Because I was deeply in love with him and committed to our marriage, I often reassured him of my commitment to him.

My first exposure to the Georgia chapter of Women in Film was an incredible experience for me. Finally, I had met my "pack"— gifted women who had committed to their own creative journeys (actors, directors, producers, costume designers, editors, etc.). My association with this organization as well as with Women in Film and Television International has provided me with a vital support network, and I am grateful for the many I am blessed to call my friends.

CRAZYMAKERS. I must give credit to Julia Cameron for coining this phrase. A "crazymaker" is someone whose personal drama grabs you like an octopus' tentacle and pulls you into a downward whirlpool. I recently experienced a crazymaker and know how difficult and trying it can be. We learn by practice to spot them and avoid them in the future at all cost.

MINE FIELD #5: TIMES & SEASONS

This particular mine field is not nefarious. I put it in this category list, however, because if we are under its pull, we will not advance on our journey. God says very plainly, "For everything there is a season, and a time for every matter under heaven" (Ecc. 3:1). There are two Greek words that are used for "season." *Kairos* refers to a period of time possessing certain characteristics and *chronos* denotes a space of time or duration of a period. Interestingly, there are only two verses in Scripture where both are used in the same text. One of them is the Ecclesiastes passage, whereas the other is found in Daniel 2:20-21: "Blessed be the name of God forever and ever, to whom belong wisdom and might. He changes times [chronos] and seasons [kairos]; he removes kings and sets up kings."

What this seems to indicate is that throughout our journeys we will arrive at pre-ordained junctures that reflect both a specific duration of time, as well as a set of predetermined characteristics. For example, when a seed is sown into the ground, there is a season that has to do with water reaching the seed, roots beginning to sprout, and those roots going deeper and deeper into the soil causing the seedling to truly take root. This season, so to speak, has a lot of activity attached to it, but all the activity is underground. We don't see what's going on there at all; we just have to trust that it is happening.

The second truth is that this "season of root-growing" involves a predetermined amount of actual time. We may see signs that the season (time) is nearing an end, but it is something clearly not in our control. Thus, if we are going through something that the Lord determines as a key season for a growth activity that will take a certain amount of time, we will not be able to bypass this season and go onto another phase in our journeys. We simply do not have the power to do that. Rhetorically speaking, whatever the Power is that "removes kings and sets up kings" is powerful enough to keep us in one spot for the rest of our lives, if He so desires. We will never be able to subdue it!

If you find yourself seemingly stuck on your journey, unable to move forward despite every attempt to do so, you may well be in the grip of the wrong time and season for you to advance. Wait and relax, for most likely, something deeper and more precious is going on internally.

MINE FIELD #6: SATAN

I have discussed this mine field earlier in this chapter as well as in Chapter 8; nonetheless, I want to underscore that we have a very personal foe who is committed to our destruction. The New Testament teaches that Satan tempts us away from our paths in three main arenas: the lust of the flesh (drugs, sex, pornography, etc.), the lust of the eyes (covetousness, greed, envy), and the pride of life (fame, recognition, self-glory) (I Jn. 2:16).

The entire book of Job was written because the devil challenged Almighty God to a show-down. Job was our forerunner of suffering. When blocked, we have to consider whether or not we are being opposed by a demonic onslaught or by something else. Sometimes the root cause is difficult to discern. I have found that in the presence of evil, there are definite signs: fear, terror, confusion, and accusations. Onslaught comes as machine gun fire and can appear relentless.

Our only recourse is to solicit the prayer of others, declare faith in the strength of the Lord's victorious right hand, and wait out the battle. I liken the experience to being on a roller coaster. When the car suddenly takes a nosedive, you know in every fiber of your soul that you are powerless to change its direction. You grip the sides, scream, and ride it out.

MINE FIELD #7: GOD

As stated earlier, God would rather take us out of the journey altogether than see us arrive with an impure heart. If you have ever had the Lord as your beloved Adversary, you know what I'm talking about. There *is* no getting around Him!

I think of the passages in 2 Samuel 6 and 1 Chronicles 14 where David was attempting to do a good thing, or so he thought. Samuel had already told David that God had appointed him to be king. Thus, David was stretching his leadership ability and attempting to bring the ark of the covenant back home to the Israelites, after it was stolen. Carrying the ark home was a big deal. David assembled all Israel together, involving a big celebration and procession. I have no doubt that David felt blessed by God that he was performing such a noble task.

Suddenly, the action shifted. The oxen that were pulling the cart, which bore the ark, stumbled and Uzzah, who had the responsibility of traveling with the ark, put out his hand and touched the ark in order to steady it. "The anger of the Lord was kindled against Uzzah; and he smote him because he put forth his hand to the ark; and he died there before God. And David was angry because the Lord had broken forth upon Uzzah...and was afraid of God that day" (1 Chron. 13:9-12).

David had gone out on a limb for God to bring the ark home. What a lofty goal, a noble one, one that surely God would bless. Not only was there no outward sign of blessing, God struck the whole effort down by slaying Uzzah. David was stopped dead in his tracks, but he made the wrong assumption. He lost face before the people, lost confidence in his leadership ability, lost assurance that he really did hear from God on whether to do this or not, and he quit his journey right there. He assumed God was no longer with him. Wrong assumption. God was not angry with David. He was angry with Uzzah's presumption and killed him on the spot. For whatever reason known only to Almighty God, He did not want Uzzah to be part of David's kingdom. The truth, which took awhile for David to realize, was: God's original purposes and destiny for David did not change.

When Joshua was leading the Israelites into battle to claim their inheritance, their first battle was at Jericho. What a triumphant victory for God's people! I have no doubt that Joshua thought to himself, "Boy, this is going to be easy! With God on our side, we can't lose!" Wrong. The next battle was at Ai, and the Israelites lost the battle soundly. They were horrified to think that God was not with them! Much soul-searching took place before the truth was uncovered: someone named Achan, within the Israelite camp, stole spoils from the battle, which had been forbidden by the Lord. Achan's greed caused the entire nation to suffer. Rather than blessing Israel, God became their Adversary.

There are times within the journey when we are blocked. There is a stone wall we cannot, under any circumstances, get around or over. Worse, it is often at these times that we cannot discern just who our adversary is: ourselves, someone else, wrong time and season, demonic opposition, or God Himself. Sometimes the blockage takes months, even years, to sort through to be able to move forward. There are no easy answers in this regard. I only know that in my own experience, God seems to reward us when we diligently seek the truth behind the blocks and trust Him to remove them in His time.

Not long ago I learned an enlightening and comforting truth from Isaiah. When the beloved prophet had his life-changing experience with God, he wrote, "Then flew one of the seraphim to me, having in his hand a burning coal which he had taken with tongs from the altar. And he touched my mouth, and said, 'Behold, this has touched your lips; your guilt is taken away, and your sin forgiven.'" (Is.. 6:6-7) Loving the prophets as I do, I pondered this passage for quite awhile and the Lord began to show me a deep truth: *He wounds the very parts of us He intends to use.*

The Lord's destiny for Isaiah was to be God's mouthpiece to His people, one who would speak for God, uphold His ways, and instruct His people in obedience and faithfulness. What part of his body, though, did the Lord allow to be burned? Isaiah's lips. I wondered what would happen if you put a hot coal to someone's lip. The searing flesh of the nerve endings of the lip, a very sensitive part of the body, would cause a ripple effect to course throughout his being. Moreover, the burn would undoubtedly leave a scar that would forever remain. Whenever Isaiah spoke on behalf of God— his destiny and calling—he would therefore always be reminded of the scar left behind by God Himself, causing him to be ever diligent to be faithful and obedient to his task. Just as Isaiah was asked to bear the Lord's marks on his body, so we may be asked to bear ours.

If you have been wounded, deeply wounded on your journey, ask yourself this: could my Adversary be God Himself? Has He wounded me in the very area in which He desires to use me?

CHAPTER 10

Survive the *Wilderness*

S ince I have spent the bulk of my life in the wilderness, allow me to share lessons or perspectives I have learned to help me survive. It is this survival quality the Lord deems most vital for our eternal wellbeing: "Count it all joy when you meet various trials, for you know that the testing of your faith produces steadfastness, And let steadfastness have its full effect, that you may be perfect and complete, lacking in nothing" (James 1:2-4). He desires us to be perfect and complete, which we cannot be if the quality of steadfastness or perseverance is lacking. Thinking back to the generation of Israelites that left Egypt on the way to Canaan, the reality was that the majority of their lives were spent only in the wilderness. Believe me, if the wilderness is to be my only lot in life, then I sure want to learn how to survive it in the way that would be pleasing to God.

Sow the seeds you've been given. One of the more discouraging passages of Scripture for me has typically been Proverbs 31, for it describes the perfect woman. One day, however, I gleaned an important nugget. "With the fruit of her hands she plants a vineyard" (Prov. 31:16). Therein lies a principle in sowing and reaping. The godly woman planted a vineyard (the end result, the harvest) from the "fruit of her hands." She couldn't very well plant a vineyard if she had a banana in her hand. She sowed from the seeds with which she had been entrusted. We each need to ask ourselves: What are the seeds I have been given? What has God placed in my hand? Those are the seeds He desires me to plant; more importantly, He expects and desires those seeds to produce fruit. This is a promise we can hold onto. Many times we look at someone else's garden and long for the seeds they were given. The focus in

Proverbs is to be on our seeds and view them as the end result: a vineyard!

The first part of verse 16 illustrates another principle: "She considers a field and buys it; with the fruit of her hands she plants a vineyard." What she did was to visualize the vineyard. She looked at the field and saw her vineyard. With that mental picture clearly fixed in her mind, she planted the seeds. This is part of the creative gifting called visualization, the ability to envision the final scene. If you do not have a clear visualization for your creative seeds, ask God for one, and drag it before your mind when the road looks bleak. God gave me the vision for *A Time To Dance.* I see what it can become. When it looks as if nothing will ever happen to it again, the exhortation is to drag out my vision, keep it before me, and continue to sow into it.

Step forward into the battle. There is an exciting story in 2 Chronicles 13. During that time the Israelites were divided following the death of Solomon—Abijah began to reign in Judah and Jereboam was king of Israel. The two kings came forth for battle. Jereboam had fallen into idolatry, whereas Abijah desired to be obedient to the Lord. The battle appeared hopeless for the Lord's warriors since Abijah and Judah were outnumbered two to one. "And when Judah looked, behold, the battle was before and behind them; and they cried to the Lord, and the priests blew the trumpets." (2 Chron. 13:14) In reality, there was absolutely nothing positive about this situation from Abijah's perspective. The outcome appeared utterly hopeless. He did not see God's hand anywhere. Is that not the way we often are in the wilderness? We don't see Him anywhere. The lesson is what happened next: "Then the men of Judah raised the battle shout. And when the men of Judah shouted, God defeated Jeroboam and all Israel before Abijah and Judah...Thus the men of Israel were subdued at that time, and the men of Judah prevailed, because they relied upon the Lord, the God of their fathers" (2 Chron. 13:15, 18).

God's victorious hand did not appear until Abijah took a step forward into the battle and gave the battle cry. God rewards our faith, our stepping forth into the battle even though everything looks hopeless. Time and time again, God shows up after we have made our move, not before.

Do what God shows YOU. Hebrews 11 is the great faith chapter, chronicling the exploits of great men and women of the faith who simply believed God and did what they were asked to do. The faith hero I identify with most is Noah. "By faith Noah, being warned by God concerning events as yet unseen, took heed and constructed an ark for the saving of his household" (Heb. 11:7). Noah does not appear in Genesis until he is 500 years old. When he entered the ark, he was six hundred. We do not know exactly how long it took him to build the ark, but it was a long time, perhaps close to 100 years. I cannot imagine the torment Noah must have gone through, not only from the people around him, making fun of him for doing something so outlandish, but it is very likely he was questioned by his family: "Dad, are you sure you heard the Lord?" Day after day, Noah was faithful to what God had told him. He was rewarded for that faith, and when the rain finally came, he was validated for his steadfastness. Noah heeded this principle: he did what God showed *him*. Furthermore, he continued to focus on that obedience day after day when he showed up for work. That's what God wants from us: total obedience to the leading and our showing up everyday for the task.

Practical ways God speaks. The Scripture is the Word of God, and how we use it in our lives is important. I need to make a distinction between two Greek words that refer to God's Word. The word *logos* refers to the unchanging, inerrant, inspired Word of God. It is the entire written Word we commonly refer to as Scripture or the Bible. When this word is used, it refers to the complete revelation of God found in the Scriptures. There is another Greek word, *rhema,* which is derived from the verb "to speak." It is used in Romans 10:17, "So faith comes by hearing, and hearing by the Word (rhema) of God." A rhema is a word or an illumination that God speaks directly to us, addressing our unique, personal situation. It is a timely, Holy Spirit inspired word from the Logos that brings life, power, and faith to do whatever He shows.

I recall an experience I had in 1993, one of those times when God's Word jumped off the pages and into my heart. In other words, my heart was emblazoned with a rhema. I was reading in Proverbs 27: "Know well the condition of your flocks, and give attention to your herds; for riches do not last for ever..." (Prov. 27:23-24). What spoke to me in this passage was that the Lord led His people to diversify, to have both flocks and herds to ensure they would be cared for in life. Whereas the flocks of sheep provided wool and meat, the goats provided milk. There was great wisdom in God's exhortation, and I began to consider it for my own life.

Flocks and herds became a new paradigm shift for me, and after spending days and weeks considering its application for my life, I decided to start my second company, Quadra Entertainment, in order to seed into my writing career. I was at the age where I needed to think about the future. Having been without a husband for much of my life, I had never developed the mindset of depending on a man to take care of me. Thus, I needed to plan for my own retirement. I knew I had been given writing gifts and had really never sowed creative seeds in that field. I was too involved in my ad agency to devote time to writing.

In 1994. I made a commitment to add herds to my flocks, with the faith that when I became older, I would be able to enjoy two income streams from two areas of giftings. This was a huge step of faith for me, for as I have said before, the step cut my income in half during the long years it has taken to sow seeds into the writing side of my life. Many times, I have questioned the call: "Did I really hear God?" "Lord, are You sure You want me to do this?" I have certainly not received the validation nor the financial rewards of these efforts. It is as if Noah is hammering away saying, "Lord, are You sure it's going to rain?"

My son, who has witnessed the many struggles involved with this effort, once handed me a quote by Mark Twain in an attempt to make me laugh: "Write without pay until somebody offers pay. If nobody offers pay within three years, the candidate may look upon this circumstance with the most implicit confidence as the sign that sawing wood is what he was intended for."

No doubt Twain would have given a similar message to Noah...yet this is our call—to walk in the shoes of Noah and be faithful to the call God has given to each one of us, trusting that one day we will be rewarded for our obedience.

Listen for the Shepherd's voice. I once heard the story of a man's experience in Israel. While visiting some of the famous biblical sites, he ran into a group of shepherds, each herding his own sheep into a round pen for the night. The same round pen. All of the sheep were mingled together, and the man wondered how in the world the shepherds would be able to separate them the next morning, since none of the sheep had any identifiable marks. The next morning, one of the shepherds came over to the pen and spoke to the sheep. One by one, the sheep filed out to follow him...only his sheep. The exact thing happened with the other two shepherds. Each sheep responded only to his shepherd's voice.

Jesus says He is our Shepherd who knows each one of us intimately. "I know my own and my own know me" (John 10:14). We learn through life to hear His voice and to follow Him when we do.

There is no set way God speaks to people. His voice is different depending on how we can best hear Him. God speaks in many ways, among them: 1) through the still small voice inside; 2) through the counsel of godly people; 3) through a personal rhema—the Holy Spirit highlighting certain Scripture and applying it to a set of circumstances in our lives; 4) through circumstances, such as doors opening or shutting; 5) through a sound mind weighing the pros and cons; 6) through dreams or visions; 7) through God's audible voice, which is rare; and 9) through the peace we experience when we have moved out in the direction of His leading.

Each one of us is different in the way we hear Him best, and His desire is to train us by practice to discern His voice from the other voices that try to invade our minds (demonic accusations, or our own selfish thoughts). I think we have all been confused at times in the walk of faith discerning His voice. If He begins speaking to me in ways I've never before experienced, such as the time following my most difficult test, I didn't hesitate talking with those far wiser and experienced in the faith walk than I. If only we had ears to hear…that was His plea on earth. The Lord's commitment and passion is to speak to His children so that we will know His abiding, personal comfort during the wilderness journey. Our part is to press in and not leave His presence until we hear Him. All too often, we give up too soon and conclude He doesn't have anything to say to us.

Accept moments of encouragement along the way. Not long ago, two women visited me in my home. One of the women I didn't know well, but she had been recommended as a very wise woman. I had sought her counsel on whether what I was hearing on a particular matter was truly from God. In other words, He was speaking to me in a new way, and I therefore sought the advice of a woman uniquely gifted in discernment. We had a lovely visit and Peggy confirmed that what I was hearing seemed very much to be the Lord's voice.

Later in the week, I ran into Peggy at a conference. She came over to me and handed me a small white box and said, "This is for you." Puzzled, I opened the box and saw a pair of long, feather-shaped silver and turquoise earrings. She then said, "When I was over at your house the other day, I heard the Lord say to me, 'Give Candace your earrings.' Not knowing you very well, I didn't do it right then. I came home and once again, the Lord said, 'I want Candace to have your earrings.'" The meaning of the gift was unclear to me. Of course I was touched by it, but I wasn't getting it. Sensing my puzzlement, Peggy explained, "The Lord told me that you needed a feather in your cap. Look at these earrings. They are comprised of six feathers. He wants you to know that you are validated in His eyes!" Tears streamed down my cheeks when I realized that the Lord had spoken something very personal to me through this woman who was experienced in hearing His voice.

Be like-minded as a shepherd. As creatives, it is easy for us to focus our creative energy on our creative children rather than our own. They are far less demanding! Nonetheless, one of the great lessons I have had on my journey is that the Lord is building into me the character trait of being a shepherd in the way that He is mine. As my Shepherd, the Lord is fiercely protective of me and goes to any lengths to listen to my cries and meet the needs I have. He has modeled for us what it takes to truly be a shepherd, in that He gave His life for His sheep. He expects us to tend our own sheep with the same dedication and self-sacrifice. So many times we are consumed with this angst that says, "My career is going nowhere! What do I do?" The answer: be content in the pasture the Lord has placed you in now. In that part of the pasture where you are fenced in, there and only there will you be fed, protected, comforted. Tend to the young lambs you have in that pasture rather than looking at somebody else's field and wanting to jump the fence. The fact remains: Jesus chose to sacrifice for His sheep rather than seek His own glory. He wants us to be like Him, and that means choosing our children's needs above our creative pursuits.

Move when God moves. When the Israelites were wandering in the wilderness, God taught them how He would lead them. When it was time for them to stop and rest, God's presence in the cloud rested over the tent of meeting. When the cloud lifted, it was time to pick up and move again. "Throughout all their journeys, whenever the cloud was taken up from over the tabernacle, the people would go onward; but if it was not taken up, then they stayed" (Ex. 40:36). God's presence was both felt and seen on a regular basis. As we learn to walk with God, we will sense when it's time to move or stay.

Some months after Mike passed away, I woke up one morning and knew it was time to move. It was time to get on with the next phase of my life. I didn't hear an audible voice, but I just knew, and I have come to trust that inner knowing. It is one of the ways God has always spoken to me. I need to say here that God always confirms His leading by two or three witnesses, in the event someone would mistakenly think that last night's burrito could be mistaken for the "voice of God"! When I get that inner knowing, I start moving out in the direction of the leading, waiting for God's confirmation signs.

I began to sort out my belongings and purge those things I no longer needed or wanted. I put the house on the market and spent much time in prayer asking for clear direction. It didn't come for several more months; to be precise, it did not come until the week my son went off to college. My house sold and I had two weeks to vacate and find a new place to live. The cloud was moving, and I had to pack in a hurry to follow it!

When we move into transition, our tendency is still to do the same things we always did, attend the same church, and go to the same functions. During this time of transition for me, I attended an industry event—one which I had attended many times before. While there, however, I felt strangely removed. I didn't feel like I "fit" anymore. That was a key sign: I didn't fit because for this particular part of the journey, His cloud had lifted. Had I remained, I would have been left behind!

Learn from the journeys of others. Just months after my financial devastation, I wrote in my journal, "I feel broke, depleted, drained, betrayed, and ignored. I know I need to give You thanks, but I feel abandoned by You." I want to say here that it is very important to lay your true feelings on the line with God. He knows our hearts anyway, and wants that level of honesty with us. That day I happened to be reading 2 Corinthians 1 and the entire passage spoke of Paul's experiences. He had been given a supernatural experience where the Lord Himself appeared to Him and commissioned him to preach to the Gentiles. He writes of his first journey: "We were so utterly, unbearably crushed that we despaired of life itself. Why, we felt that we had received the sentence of death" (2 Cor. 1:8). He continues, "We are afflicted in every way, but not crushed; perplexed, but not driven to despair; persecuted, but not forsaken; struck down, but not destroyed; always carrying in the body the death of Jesus, so that the life of Jesus may also be manifested in our bodies" (2 Cor. 4:8-10).

I was impressed to look at the routes of Paul's travels, and was enlightened and encouraged that the above passages referred to his first journey. In all, Paul had four journeys or ventures. His first one was the shortest, and the one that almost broke him. Though he was on the verge of being destroyed, he was not. Hope, for me, came in realizing that Paul had a second journey, which was longer. He got further this time, preached in more towns, and began to flow in the giftings, strength, and power God had given him for his task. I stared at the map showing the length of each of Paul's journeys and how his effectiveness increased the more he stepped out in faith.

Too often, I believe, we lose heart after our first journey out in our calling. I encourage you to visualize Paul's paths, and realize that your second journey will be easier, for you will have been strengthened by the first one to operate more fully in your giftings in the second, and the third, etc.

Realize some have a rougher journey than others. There is no getting around this truth. It has perplexed me for years because it seems so unfair. Worse, if you're one of the ones whose road has been harder, then it's tempting to imagine that there is some horrible sin that lurks in your life and you're not worthy for anything else other than a hard road!

Malachi 3, however, tells an entirely different story: "Who can endure the day of his (the Lord's) coming, and who can stand when he appears? For he is like a refiner's fire...he will sit as a refiner and purifier of silver, and he will purify the sons of Levi and refine them like gold and silver, till they present right offerings to the Lord" (Mal. 3:2-3).

There are several wonderful truths in this passage. What does a refiner of silver do? Silver must be refined by fire to rid it of dross and impurities. Only then is it of value and worth. Only then can it be molded and shaped by the silversmith. There's the classic tale of someone who asked a silversmith, "Do you sit by the fire watching the refining process?" He replied, "Yes, of course. If I didn't watch it very carefully, the fire could easily destroy the silver." "But how do you know when the refining process is finished?" The silversmith smiled and said, "Oh, that's easy. When I can see my reflection in the silver."

God holds us carefully in the refining fire and watches ever so closely until the process produces a mirror image of Him. Notice, however, another insight often overlooked. God didn't perform this refining process on everyone, only on the Levites. Why the Levites? Because they were the ones who had been especially set apart from the rest of His children to perform ministry and service to Him. Theirs was the responsibility to "present right offerings before Him," to come before His presence and offer prayers and sacrifices on behalf of the people and lead them in worship and teach them to walk in His ways.

If you look around and see that your life has been tougher than most, most likely you have been set apart as a Levite, as unto the Lord and His work. If you have, then you can expect the refining fire to be turned up for you, but take comfort in the calling that is yours. Levites are not any more special to God than others. However, their calling to be in closer proximity to the holiness of God requires them to undergo the painful extraction of self-centered impurities.

CHAPTER 11

When the *Vision* Dies

Robert (not his real name) was a man who walked with God. One day God gave him a huge vision, that of opening a Christian nightclub in a well-known resort town. The vision was a noble one, for Robert's' motivation was to provide a different kind of entertainment and offer an alternative for families who did not want to get lured away by typical nightclub resort fare. Robert wanted the world to see that God's ways were different and reach people for the Lord who wouldn't normally be found inside a church. A charismatic individual, Robert was so impassioned for his vision that he easily gathered around him a group of investors who shared his dream. Together, with Robert's faith and the investors' money, they would begin to change the world for the Lord, one resort town at a time. Everything was going along fine until the vision died.

Robert's venture began to lose money. He stepped up his prayer efforts, called forth God's army of prayer warriors but to no avail. He was soon forced to shut the doors, and the investors lost all their money. Robert's faith was shaken. Where was God? Did he even hear Him at all when the vision first burst into his soul?

I wish I could report this as an isolated incident. Unfortunately it is not. In fact, at this writing, I know ten people who are undergoing this very same scenario. All are devout men and women who have noble visions and have gone out on a limb and laid it on the line for God. All are watching their visions die. I know this experience well because I have lived it.

WHAT IS A VISIONARY?

I've given this question a lot of thought, especially after my own vision died. Such a death causes you to re-assess everything you have ever thought, to see where possibly you went wrong and what you can do to correct the "way you see" so it doesn't trip you up again.

What I have come to believe is that the "visionary" gift is truly that: a gift. To be a visionary means that you have the ability to see the big picture. Within the mind comes a flash of inspiration that is a panorama of the calling—a panorama that is forevermore imprinted in the visionary's brain and drives all his actions. John Sandford, in his classic book *The Elijah Task*, describes this gift as it operates in prophetic individuals: "The prophet often knows the end of a scene, only to find that he knows nothing in between, and life may not go as he has seen it at all."[12]

This "end scene" imprint is not given just to prophets. Rather, God dispenses it to men and women in all occupations. Isaiah describes this divine attribute very succinctly: "I am God, and there is none like me, declaring the end from the beginning and from ancient times things not yet done, saying 'My counsel shall stand, and I will accomplish all my purpose'" (Isa. 46:9-10). Seeing the final scene is a divine attribute, part of the divine DNA that has fallen to the visionary. However, whereas God has given visionaries the "final scene," He has not gifted us to know the scenes in the middle. We are thus forced to walk by faith like everyone else.

God not only knows the final scene, but all the scenes leading up to it. "For my thoughts are not your thoughts, neither are your ways my ways, says the Lord. For as the heavens are higher than the earth, so are my ways higher than your ways and my thoughts than your thoughts" (Isa. 55:8-9). Paul refers to our human "middle-scene deficiency" when he says, "Now I know in part; then I shall understand fully..." (I Cor. 13:12). The most difficult thing for visionaries, however, is that because we often attract others to share our vision, we are therefore called into the excruciating consequence of not only watching the vision die ourselves, but having scores of other people see us go down in flames!

LETTING GO

The only way a plant has a chance to grow is by letting go of the seed, burying it, and walking away. If you go back out the next day and dig it up, just to see if it's grown any, you destroy its chances for life. It has to be buried for its pre-determined time (or season). Only then will it grow. It has to die to its "seedness" (i.e., its infancy stage) in order to be transformed into the magnificent new growth it was always intended to be.

We creative sowers see so much potential in our special seed (or "vision"), be it a script, a piece of art, an acting career, a poem, or an entrepreneurial venture. We see what it can become, and to us that seed is the most precious thing in the world. We see its full growth potential, and we hold it in the palm of our hand and say, "Isn't it lovely?" The world looks at it and shrugs, "It's just a seed" and walks away. We run after them as if to say, "Don't you see it? It's magnificent! It will be a box office killer!" And still they look at what is, to them, just like every other seed. Only once in a miracle will someone else be given a glimpse of what you see in that seed and want to nurture it too. But it seldom happens.

Instead, others walk away, and suddenly you look at that seed and realize you are the only one to whom is given the ability to see what it can become. That means you and only you are its sower because to you and you alone that seed was given. You've carried it around for years and marveled at its wonder, dragging it out to put on display when someone new walks into your life. You'll do anything but the one thing you must do, to see if it is destined to grow.

YOU HAVE TO WALK AWAY

You have to bury the thing, turn your back, and walk away. My creative journey has involved many such graveside services. One of my first big ones was when I was called on to bury my music dreams. For 12 years that seed was buried, until the resurrection of *A Time To Dance*, when all of a sudden new interest blossomed forth over my music.

In April 2000, I experienced another "death of a vision"—three major blows to my career pursuits occurred back to back: prospects for a book deal died, a pending movie deal with a television network fell through, and my plans to re-locate to L.A. crumbled. My creative vision died. My life as I knew it was over. Just weeks later, I was in meetings to produce the musical. On that occasion, the burial season was short.

My most recent experience is the one I am undergoing as I write this book. I've discussed various aspects about producing *A Time To Dance*, the excitement and promise of it, the trials during the production itself, how moved the audiences were, and the rave reviews of the music. What I did not mention was that its World Premiere was scheduled for September 11, 2001.

In one fell swoop, on one dark day in the history of America, my "dream" was torpedoed too. I had no choice but to postpone opening night for three days, but that cut our scheduled performances down from thirteen to eight, an automatic loss of 40% of box office potential. For the first four performances, audiences were afraid to come, fearing Atlanta was the next target. All told, we estimate that we lost 70% of our potential box office.

The test then became much more personal. Shutting the show down and declaring bankruptcy was not an option for me, for then my investors would never have a chance to re-coup. The only choice I had was to continue that second week, but to do so required substantial capital. With no hopes of box office, we didn't have it. My personal test got tougher. I chose to personally guarantee these emergency lines of credit out of my own pocket. Our only hope was to expose the show ("look at the seed!") to as many potential producers, investors, and sponsors as we could.

Audiences loved the show. It was very inspirational and healing during America's greatest crisis. More and more we all saw its potential. We kept and still keep the vision. The reality, however, was more cruel. At the show's end, I was personally devastated financially, stripped of much of my inheritance, and all of my savings.

As I write this, I do have the comfort of knowing that I did what I believe I was called to do. Following the premiere, I contacted our creditors and explained the situation and asked their patience as we attempted to reconcile our indebtedness. I produced a video and advertising piece and sent it to licensing producers looking for black musicals to tour. One of my producers took it to the film industry for consideration. I've had to dig in and attempt to re-structure my life financially. And finally, I've had to relinquish the vision yet again, bury the seed and walk away, so to speak. I have done all I know to do. The rest is in God's hands, and in the genetic pre-determination of the seed. If it is meant to be, then it will be re-born in its season.

This has been the hardest creative trial of all, for not only did it encompass my creativity, it engulfed whatever financial stability and professional reputation I thought I had. God knows wherein we need to be tested. For me, it was here. Never before had I ventured so far out on the limb. Never before were my financial resources so involved in the risk. But it's been here that I was reminded of another divine truth: "What you sow does not come to life until it dies" (1 Cor. 15:36). Every seed that you sow—every talent you've given your all for, every business plan you've developed, every friend that you've loved, every family member you've poured your life into—everything that you have ever sown does not come to life until it dies. True art, if it is meant to grow, must die. And as its sower, you have to relinquish it.

DON'T GIVE UP

That said, however, we are nonetheless called on to remain steadfast to our particular journeys, and do the next thing on today's path. Everything I am writing about in this book, I am living out during this present test. I am having to stand firm against the onslaught of negative doubts and cries of doom. Each day I have to refuse to bow my knee to the fear of the unknown, to financial ruin, to the inability to bring a return to my investors who believed so strongly in me.

One day I was touched by Psalm 16:5: "The Lord is my chosen portion and my cup." I read it over and over. Our chosen portion and our cup is all any of us need for any given day. The psalmist says the Lord is to be all we need, not box office receipts, a huge licensing fee from a touring producer, or a corporate backer to finance a road tour. With this trial, I am learning the full impact of this psalm. I have had to trust in God's provision in a way I've never had to trust before, experiencing day by day His steadfast love, both of which have come to me in incredible ways.

One day I was crying about my circumstances—I did that a lot! My son overheard me and said, "What's the matter, Mom, are we broke?" Not wanting to burden him, I replied, "It's a tough time, son, but I don't want you to worry. Just pray. The Lord will see us through." I had declared God's faithfulness, but I still needed to cry some more. The grief had to come out. I went downstairs to the kitchen sink—a familiar crying place—and let it all out. Just then Tyler walked back in the room and held out his hand, "Mom, here's $75, will this help?" Tears gushed forth even more by his sweet sensitivity. I gave him a hug and said, "Yes, son, it will help. Thank you." It was difficult, but the Lord thought it time to let my 17-year-old carry some of the load. That $75 bought groceries that week.

To say the next months were trying would be a gross understatement. All of my available cash was gone. I did not want to go to my family for help, though they would have graciously offered. Rather, I believed God had allowed this to happen. He tells us, "In everything give thanks, for this is the will of God for you in Christ Jesus" (I Thess. 5:18). That means even in my desperation I was to give thanks and to continue to look to Him in faith. He had always promised to be my Provider. I needed to depend on Him to be so now. One of my favorite passages has been, "God is the God of the fatherless, and the protector of widows." I was a widow, and I needed to see His provision, and His protection.

My attentions turned to my ad agency once again. The late John Hammer, President of Cornelia Textiles, had come with his family to the musical and told me he needed a new brochure. I told him I couldn't help him right then, thinking of course the musical would take off on its national circuit. After the premiere's devastation, I called him and said, "John, do you still need that brochure? I will gladly do it. I need the work." After our initial consult for the job, I turned to walk away when he said, "Wait a minute. Here this is your retainer for the job." I stared down at the thousand dollar check and tears rolled down my cheeks. God was proving Himself faithful and working through this dear man.

How well I remember the many days I was terrified to go to the mailbox because I did not want to see any more bills. Daily I was on my face before the Lord, pleading for Him to come to my aid. One day I finally got up the courage and went to the mailbox. Inside were three letters: the first was from a dear friend who said, "You are such an inspiration for your faithfulness to the Lord. I am praying for you!" The next letter was from my pastor's wife, assuring me of her prayers along with a check for a hundred dollars. The final letter came from a man in my church whom I hardly knew. He wrote that when he found out what had happened to me, God would not let it leave him alone all day! He wrote, "I hope this will not offend you, but I believe the Lord wanted me to give this to you." Inside was a check for a thousand dollars.

Day by day the Lord provided for me in unbelievable ways. He provided a buyer for my home, enabling me to pay off a $50,000 loan that was due that very month. He led me to the place where I was to move. The minute I walked inside, I knew it. One week later, a piece of property my family had had for years—property that we had been totally unable to sell—suddenly sold and with the portion of the sale I was given, I was able to furnish my new home. Those closest to me, especially my son, witnessed firsthand God's incredible provision. David says it so beautifully, "I have been young, and now am old; yet I have not seen the righteous forsaken or his children begging bread. He is ever giving liberally and lending, and his children become a blessing" (Ps. 37:25-26). God proves Himself faithful to those who declare Him to be, even in the face of adversity. Over and over, the Scriptures speak of God's steadfast love and faithfulness to His children, those who are totally dependent upon Him.

When Paul was in prison, I'm sure he must have felt totally blocked in what he was called to do. Yet, that prison did not deter him. In fact, if it had not been for the prison, we would never have the bulk of the New Testament, for he used his imprisonment to write letters to the various churches. Sharing the reality and power of Jesus has changed far more lives by his written words than he could ever have done preaching in town after town.

Understanding this perspective was what actually inspired this book. I began to turn my attention to helping others, encouraging their journeys rather than complaining, staying depressed, and feeling sorry for myself. We each have that choice.

CAREFULLY EXAMINE THE DEFEAT

One day I was asking the Lord to show me if I had done something wrong in my inaugural production venture. The still voice inside said, "Read Joshua 7." The historical context of this passage is the period of time when Joshua was just beginning to lead the Israelites to conquer their promised land. They had had one triumphant battle, Jericho, where the walls miraculously fell down and the city was captured. Chapter 7 recounts their second battle, Ai, where they experienced horrific defeat. Joshua fell on his face before the Lord pleading for enlightenment. You know the story: God showed him that something was not done right at Jericho and because of that error, they were blocked from success at the subsequent battle of Ai. This is an important principle: if we experience blockage and an inability to go forward, check the previous venture to see if something went amiss.

Joshua's destiny was still to lead God's people into the Promised Land. Yet he was being blocked. He had to take time to search out the root of the blockage. As I was reading this passage, I thought, "Oh, I see...there was someone in my 'camp' that you wanted removed before going forward." In other words, I was still looking at myself as blameless. Every time I thought I understood the passage, the Lord would put a check in my spirit, "No, you still haven't seen it. Look at it again. Press in for My truth."

Joshua was forced to press in too. God said to him, "You cannot stand before your enemies until you take away the devoted things from among you" (Josh. 7:13). What had happened was that God had ordered His people to totally destroy everything in Jericho. It was dedicated to destruction, and all the spoils were to be given to the Lord. Achan had stolen a mantle, silver, and gold from Jericho and hidden them under his tent. God had Joshua seek out those things, and destroy Achan and his entire family.

I still didn't understand. The Lord kept pointing to the phrase "devoted for destruction" and slowly the revelation began to unfold. God intended for them to take away nothing from the battle for themselves. Now, if God gave you a major assignment and said, "By the way, I expect you to come away with nothing for all your efforts," that would be a tough pill to swallow, wouldn't it? Why even bother to venture out at all? Therein is our lesson.

EVERYBODY NEEDS A JERICHO

Jericho was the Israelites' first battle. The way they handled it was critical to the eventual success of the entire taking of their land (their destiny). They would have died right at Ai if they hadn't purged what was not right and pure before God. In like manner, we must get through our Jerichos successfully if we are to proceed onto our destiny.

I cannot apply this principle to your life. I can only reveal what God showed me in mine at this particular point. God wanted me to see that He desired that I take away no spoils from my production venture. *A Time To Dance* was His, and all the spoils from my personal efforts He intended to put into His treasury. Ouch. "Lord, do you mean I'm to take away absolutely nothing from this venture?" That's precisely what He was telling me to do: lay my Jericho down and all the things I hoped to get. That day He laid my heart bare before Him, and I was no better than Achan. What I had hoped to get from my venture was business prestige, material success, backing for the next project, and a higher rung on the entertainment producers' ladder. He whispered, "Those are the things that are devoted for destruction."

God's purpose for me was to destroy my "right to the spoils," which in essence was Achan's sin. At any time Achan could pull out that beautiful mantle from Shinar and boast to himself and his children, "I got this during the battle at Jericho!" Our rights to the spoils include all those prideful things we want for ourselves: the fame, recognition, awards, trophies, and royalties. We want to parade our Jerichos, bring out a momento or an award and say, "Aren't I something!"

What I was eventually shown was to divert all my future earnings in *A Time To Dance*, if there are to be any, to what the Lord has shown me to do with them, which is to help others. He wanted to teach me a principle of "first fruits," of dedicating the first harvest of my creative seed as a writer/producer totally to the Lord's treasury. He was saying to me, "*A Time To Dance* was never meant to be yours. I brought it in and out of your life to see what you would do with it. You kept trying to benefit from it, but it is Mine to show forth My glory and to be used for My purposes." I would never have seen this important principle had my venture not been derailed, and had I not been finally open to hear whatever He might show me, even though the lesson was painful.

WHAT ARE FIRST FRUITS?

The concept of "first fruits" goes back to the time of harvest when the Israelites were instructed to bring the first of the harvest to the altar and sacrifice them to God in thanksgiving and in recognition of His Lordship and bounty. God clearly told Joshua that everything in Jericho was to be His, but in all subsequent battles, the people were free to enjoy the spoils. God wanted the principle to be strongly fixed in His peoples' hearts (and in ours): the spoils of our first efforts are to be His. The rest of our lives, we are free to enjoy the fruit of our labor.

Months later, after running into so many other people who were going through similar crises in their ventures, I again asked, "Lord, help me understand why so many of your people are getting derailed. Why are they being destroyed?" He whispered once again, "Joshua 7." I said, "Lord, I've been there. I've seen what You showed me, how we are caught up in the desire for glory and to have our fleshly needs met." He said, "Look deeper...look from another angle."

I went back to the passage and forced myself to look at it from my right brain, then my left, and tried to get a broader picture. Finally I saw it: a calculated strategy for derailment. It was the pattern (strategy) God wanted me to see, not the individual steps, but the pattern:

#1- Vision
#2- Strategy
#3- First Effort (the test)
#4- Victory (and flesh is tainted with self-glory)
#5- Loss

The sober reality is that most of us cannot get past our Jerichos. It is after Step #5 that I believe Napoleon Hill was referring when he said that 95% of people turn back. God allows this loss because our fleshly desires will never fit us for the ultimate victory and God's glory. We need to also see, however, that God's ultimate intention was for Joshua and His people to keep going. He still had the Promised Land as their destiny. In like manner, we have to know that God has a wonderful destiny for us as well, but He is nonetheless committed to preventing us from ever getting there if we are not fit for the calling.

LESSONS IN RELINQUISHMENT

God called Abraham to sacrifice his only son, Isaac. You know the story, but think of it this way: God was not free to provide the substitute for the offering until Abraham showed his willingness to relinquish the right to his son and be obedient to what God asked him to do. Something miraculous happens once we get out of the way and take that important step of relinquishment.

WORSHIP IN THE MIDST OF PAIN. In I Samuel 30, King David and his army were away, faithfully serving the Lord on a mission, when suddenly enemies came into his city and stole everything: wives, children, and belongings, and burned the city. When David and his men returned, they were devastated at their personal loss. His men even turned against him, complaining that he had caused them to lose everything. "But David strengthened himself in the Lord his God" (1 Sam. 30:6). In his time with God, the Lord inspired him and guided him into what to do next: fight for what was his and take it back from the enemy. When times were tough, after David worshipped God, he was given the next step.

CROSSROADS OF THE DIVINE. We are closest to the Divine at the greatest moments of personal agony. Jesus' crucifixion is the perfect example of this principle. His physical pressure and suffering were more intense toward the end. His deepest agony was at the point of crucifixion when the Father took His Son's earthly body and put it to death for our sins. Many times He leads us to do the same as creatives: put to death all that is worldly in us—the desire for fame, wealth, and the pride of life—in order to become empty vessels for His work, not ours.

At the point of crucifixion, Jesus experienced a separation from the Father. During my deepest sorrow after the premiere, what hurt the most was a sense of separation from God. I kept asking where He was. The silence from heaven is deafening. Others close to Jesus turned away and returned to their own lives. He was left hanging there to die alone. He was powerless to do anything because He had made a choice to yield Himself fully to the Father. His last words were, "It is finished. Father, into your hands I commit my spirit." He relinquished. We are called to do nothing less.

RESURRECTION PROMISE. One day I was blowing leaves in the yard. In the back the leaves had piled up at least two feet. I forced the blower to move the pile, to make room for still more leaves. Suddenly, as two feet of leaves moved, there was a bright green lily underneath. I was shocked to see something so green and alive buried beneath dead leaves but therein was a visual reminder that what may appear to be dead, holds within it the promise of resurrection.

Death is very real in the scheme of life. For Christians, the meaning is deeply spiritual, for we know that there came the glory of the resurrection and the hope of eternal life only after Jesus' death.

For the creative, the same hope exists. When our calling has been crucified and buried, we have to have faith that if those seeds are destined for something more, they will be resurrected. That is the promise. That is the difference between those things that are "called" and those things that are "chosen." Only God knows which category we are in. That's why we should follow the path we are on and accept what comes, with thanksgiving.

During the production, when the financial situation loomed heavily on my mind, I tried to begin each day with the prayer, "Father, I accept whatever comes from your hands today." At times of relinquishment, that is the only thing we can do.

People ask me if I believe the musical is dead. No, in my heart I do not, but I clearly know its true destiny is not in my control. I believe it is undergoing yet another crucifixion and burial. I know for a certainty, though, that I do not regret for one moment the decision I made to produce it. The lessons I have learned have been priceless, worth far more than whatever I lost financially. If the musical is meant to have further life, it will be resurrected, at the right time and season. If it is not, then I believe God will shed additional light as I proceed with my creative journey.

CHAPTER 12

When You *Make It*

These two remaining chapters are different from all the others in that I have not experienced either of them yet. I feel totally confident in writing them, however, because the same God who enlightened His principles for all the preceding chapters—that I have personally experienced—is fully able to instruct us for the latter parts of the creative journey. We trust these principles by faith, faith in the surety of His Word and His will to perform it in our lives, if we continue to walk in faith. "Faith is the assurance of things hoped for, the conviction of things not seen" (Heb. 11:1). I am assured because of the trustworthiness of God and His Word that if we have been diligent to continue the path, to persevere daily, to be steadfast to walk with Him and spend time with Him, we will make it!

LOOK FOR THE HARVEST

Remember the Ecclesiastes principle: "In everything there is a season." One of those seasons is the harvest, the time when we reap what we have sown. In fact, one of the predominant series of feasts and festivals for the Israelites throughout history is the Feast of Tabernacles, or the Feast of the Ingathering. Celebrating the harvest is a time of rejoicing and praise when all our efforts pay off. The "law of the seasons" is a promise from Almighty God Himself: if we have cared for the seed, watered it, nurtured it, protected it against weeds and thorns, given it time to "do its thing," it will produce the intended fruit. We *will* receive the promised harvest.

Harvest may represent many things. For some, harvest may mean reaping great wealth for seeds sown in a risky venture. For others, harvest means walking down the aisle with the relationship you have poured months and perhaps years of your life into. For still others, harvest may be doing the best you can day by day, ful-filling your responsibilities, and being good stewards of what you have been entrusted with, and hearing, "Well done, faithful ser-vant" after you die. It may not come in the exact form you may carry in your mind, but have no fear, harvest will come.

For me, the release has been to relinquish not only my efforts, but also the outcome—my expectation of how God is going to fulfill the law of the harvest in my life, especially regarding *A Time To Dance.* Sure, he knows my desire. But I do trust that He has my best interests in mind, as well as those of my creative team and my investors.

Blessed is the man...whose delight is in the law of the Lord, and on his law he meditates day and night. He is like a tree planted by streams of water, that yields its fruit in its season, and its leaf does not wither. In all that he does, he prospers (Ps. 1:1-3).

What a wonderful promise of harvest! In its season, every seed that has been sown according to God's direction and with His nur-turing, has the promise of yielding fruit in its season. At the perfect time, the branches are strong and the tree is healthy at its core. The proper nutrients have been circulating in the depth of the tree over time, forcing its roots deep within the soil. Fruit is the natural, universal result. It's God's way and His delight for there to be fruit that enrich those who have taken part in its care.

As creatives, He wants our lives to be enriching for others, pro-viding sustenance, shelter, and a sense of stability—all those things that a healthy tree provides for its fruit. The promise of prosperity could mean money, but I think that's a stretch in this analogy. Prosperity, to me, means the inner fulfillment of knowing you are doing what you were created to do. If you are meant to be a tree, then a prosperous tree is one that is sturdy, healthy, fruit-bearing, and at one in the ecological balance of things. The same is true for us.

THE SOURCE OF NOURISHMENT

Notice in Psalm 1 on the previous page that the way to be nourished in order to guarantee the growth, the fruit, the non-withering leaves, and the prosperity, is to delight in the law of the Lord. If you have not developed the practice of regularly reading the Bible, I can only encourage you to begin. It never ceases to illumine my way. David says, "Thy Word is a lamp to my feet and a light to my path" (Ps. 119:105). It's true. Because the Bible is the Word of God, that Word is alive and His Spirit uses it to speak directly to what we need at any given time: to warn us, give us perspective and wisdom, illumine our journey, and remind us of His goodness and how special we are to Him.

THE LAW OF MULTIPLYING CROPS

In the audiotape series *The Science of Success*, Napoleon Hill explains that in everything we do, nature recognizes the law of increase. The farmer plows the field, fertilizes it, puts fences around it, and plants a seed of wheat. All at no income and at great expense. What nature does (one of God's universal laws) is to take over from there and return a crop a hundredfold, to compensate the farmer for all the hard work he put in. Hill says, "If he planted one seed of wheat and reaped only one wheat stalk, that would hardly be worth his effort." The principle is that in one way or another we will be rewarded and compensated for our efforts by multiplying the fruit.

THE LAW OF APPLIED FAITH

Understanding Hill's Law of Applied Faith became the cornerstone of what transformed me from a dreamer to a doer, from an ungrounded creative to a visionary writer/producer. It was that moment when it became clear what I was to do, not just what I *wanted* to do, but was *created* to do. Arriving at the understanding of this vital creative principle took time, but clearly the turning point was when I became convinced there was something inside blocking my ability to succeed. Change resulted when I made the decision to track it and stare it down.

In early 1998, I was on the board of Women in Film/Atlanta, and one of our members, actress Sarah Tinnon, sent out announcements that she was going to be leading an *Artist's Way* support group for those who were interested. That announcement would not leave me alone—a signal that I was to pay attention to. The last thing I had was time to venture forth on yet another non-paying exercise. But the inner voice was relentless.

The accountability that the group brought was key, I believe, to all of us working through our issues. One week, the source of my creative blockage finally surfaced. Julia Cameron writes of clarifying our personal vision,

> What we are talking about seems to be a conscious partnership in which we work along slowly and gradually, clearing away the wreckage of our negative patterning, clarifying the vision of what it is we want, learning to accept small pieces of that vision from whatever source and then, one day, presto! The vision seems to suddenly be in place. In other words, pray to catch the bus, then run as fast as you can. For this to happen, first of all, we must believe that we are allowed to catch the bus.[13]

When the group reconvened, I confessed my struggle with the assignment. I could not say for a certainty that "I was allowed to catch the bus." The more I thought about it, the more troubled I became. I had known too many people who were godly students of the Bible, gifted people, full of integrity, who battled with adversity after adversity and creative miscarriages. Who was I to think I had a right to the bus? What about them?

My "block" was a spiritual confusion—one which, I believe, has crippled many creative Christians. The great faith chapter describes faith as "the assurance of things hoped for, the conviction of things not seen" (Heb.11:1). God wants us to have assurance and conviction about things, not uncertainty. I clearly believed that what pleases God is faith, but did I have faith that God wanted me to be a writer/producer? No. I wasn't 100% certain. I knew that was my desire, but I could not be certain that was His destiny for me.

Therein lay my problem and the source of my block: the Law of Applied Faith was not operational. Allow me to retrace for a moment: remember we said before that if you put a pumpkin seed into the ground, you have complete faith that with proper water, fresh air, and sun, you will get a pumpkin. Your faith is completely operational. That same law of faith is to be applicable to our lives as well.

Paul says, "Do not be conformed to this world, but be transformed by the renewal of your mind, that you may prove what the will of God is, that which is good, and acceptable, and perfect" (Rom. 12:2). In other words, God wants to realign our thinking about ourselves and our multitudinous self-limitations, and transform us. But that can only be done by renewing our minds so that we see ourselves and our destinies from His perspective and not our own. Please note the verb tense of the command:"be transformed." It is first of all a command, the imperative form of the verb. It is not an option if we want to experience God's plan for our lives. Secondly, it is passive tense, not something we are capable of doing for ourselves. It is to be done by God Himself, but He will only do it when our minds are fixed on Him and not our own self-limiting thoughts and negative belief structures.

My revelation continued:

I bid every one among you not to think of himself more highly than he ought to think, but to think with sober judgment, each according to the measure of faith which God has assigned him (Rom. 12:3).

The key lies in our faith and the fact that transforming faith has everything to do with the way we think about ourselves. Hill's Law of Applied Faith clearly has scriptural basis. In its mathematical equation, it would read as follows:

DESIRE + FAITH = REALIZATION

That's the formula. When our faith is not operative, when we have a wrong view of ourselves, or haven't taken the time to properly assess our strengths, weaknesses, talents, gifts, and motivational patterns, then the pattern—God's pattern—is off kilter and we will not become or actualize our destiny. Conversely, when we know ourselves fully, embrace the gifts, talents, and strengths given to us, we are able to verbalize and declare our greatest desire. When we finally marry that with the type of faith that is the "assurance of things hoped for," then we will become what God put in each of our hearts to become. When we meet adversity along the way, that is nature's way of refining the call and building perseverance in our characters. Furthermore, when we have that inner assurance, we can keep going amidst adversity.

One other principle I want to point out is the phrase "according to the measure of faith which God has assigned him." God assigns an inner image of what we most desire and gives us the faith to believe we can become that thing. It would be foolish for me to say, "My desire is to be the Queen of England." The measure of faith necessary to actualize that destiny has not been given or assigned to me. There is something inside us which knows for a certainly that what we desire and believe in our hearts, we truly can and should be.

I reached a point in my journey where the Law of Applied Faith became clear. When I saw it, I verbally embraced it, saying, "Lord, I accept the work you have for me to do as a writer/producer. I look forward to see You at work as I move out to do it."

THE POWER OF VISUALIZATION

When the Israelites arrived at the edge of their promised territory, Joshua issued a command that carries with it a powerful lesson for us today.

How long will you be slack to go in and take possession of the land, which the Lord, the God of your fathers, has given you? Provide three men from each tribe, and I will send them out that they may set out and go up and down the land, writing a description of it with a view to their inheritances, and then come to me (Josh. 18:2-4).

Take possession of the land. Notice the verb tense in the above Scripture: "God *has given* you." It did not matter that other nations and peoples were already occupying the land. God clearly referred to this land as their inheritance. This land was what rightfully belonged to them as God's people. He desired that it be inhabited by those who walked in His ways, to provide the model for the rest of us that God's blessings come to those who honor Him and walk in obedience to His Laws.

Allow me to digress for a moment, for recently I was impressed by this principle anew. This one tribe of people left Egypt with a total slave mentality. They had no idea how to conquer new ground, exercise dominion, and rule as God intended. In the wilderness, through Moses, God taught them how to approach Him, how to walk with Him, how to believe in His presence, how to expect His miracles, and how to trust in His steadfast love, daily provision, and protection.

With this knowledge and faith, the Israelites became the most powerful nation on the face of the earth. What God taught them spread, and together with the advent of Christ and His followers, ultimately changed the face of Europe, Asia, and was the cornerstone of the founding of the United States. We have the privilege of living in a nation with more wealth, prosperity, and blessings than other nations of the world because our forefathers swore allegiance to a holy God and desired to walk in His ways and honor Him. Early in our history, believers in this God and His ways (first learned by the Israelites in the wilderness) had possession of all the major institutions in our country: the government, schools, orphanages, and hospitals. Slowly, though, we became "fat" on God's blessings and gave over this inheritance to others who chose not to walk in God's ways. What I see taking place in this day and hour is that God is raising up men and women of vision, who are possessed with a renewed fervor to honor Him and follow Him, and He is directing them to "take back their inheritance." There is an unprecedented call to revival, to take back our land!

Walk the land. God's instruction to Joshua was to have all 12 tribes send out representatives to "walk the land." There is a powerful connection between walking the land and visualizing it as theirs, letting the creative energy flow as to what they would do with it. In visualization, we set our imaginations to work as to what we would build, and we picture ourselves in a particular setting. The creative energy is mysteriously set free through visualization. It is one of God's key preparatory tools which increases desire and motivation, and empowers our internal sense of destiny. It is here many times that creatives fall apart. We sense that there is more we are to do in our lives, but we are often too scattered to do anything concrete. We do not have an action plan. Our desires are not refined. We have so many projects that are just "out there." We are not anywhere near close enough to be able to visualize anything because the place that holds our inner beacon is too fluid and shapeless. We have not crystallized and transfixed our destinies.

Joshua gave the people specific instructions: go out and walk the land, write down their visions, and bring them back to him. He wanted to see what they would do with their individual inheritances. In like manner, God desires to see what we would do with ours. We are each challenged to visualize what it is that we are to do, set our imaginations to it, write it down, bring it before God, consecrate it to Him, and then go to work and take the necessary action steps to move forward.

Producing *A Time To Dance* myself in 2001 was relatively easy for me to visualize because I had been through the entire process in 1989. I was totally involved in the auditioning process and the rewrites, observed every rehearsal and how the producer handled individual crises that arose. When the time came to be obedient to the directive for me to produce it, I first went to the venue we had chosen. Walking through row after row of empty seats, I pictured the performance in my mind from the various vantage points. I stood on the stage, first looking out and seeing the imaginary audience, then turning around and picturing the set, the costumes, and the characters coming to life. I acquainted myself with every part of the physical land (dressing rooms, green room, prop room, backstage, musicians pit, audio booth, lighting grid, spotlights). As I walked out the myriad business and financial details leading up to the premiere, I continued to be motivated by that inner visualization.

RECOGNIZE THE PROMISED LAND

There came a time in the Israelites' history where the season of the wilderness ended, and they arrived at their promised land. Likewise, in the creative journey, we will eventually move out of the wilderness period, and a new part of the journey will begin.

Let's look at some of the lessons and principles we can glean from our Israelite forefathers.

Let go of the wilderness mentality. The Israelites that Joshua led into the land had only experienced the wilderness. So it is for many of us. We begin to build a mental attitude that says, "I'll never receive anything. I'll never make it. Poor and needy and wandering is all I'll ever be."

This wilderness mentality is a powerful stronghold that we need to pull down and dismantle. First, though, we need to examine ourselves to see if we have one. We need to ask ourselves, "What has been my personal experience with prosperity and abundance?" Not that long ago as I was meditating on this principle, God began to show me mine. When I was growing up, my parents struggled to keep up with the Joneses, but never quite made it. Whereas my friends wore name-brand clothes, I had to make do with the look-alike brand. How well I remember those days of shame and embarrassment. As a result, I grew up seeing myself as never measuring up, always being second-best, thinking others were somehow more favored, special, or loved than I was.

Those inner strongholds, are hard to dismantle. What I had to do was to "renew my mind" and study God's view on the subject. Just exactly what does our heavenly Father say that He will provide for His children? "In all that he does he prospers" (Ps. 1:3). "The blessing of the Lord makes rich, and he adds no sorrow to it" (Prov. 10:22). "How abundant is Thy goodness, which thou hast laid up for those who fear thee, and wrought for those who take refuge in thee" (Ps. 31:19).

Our God is not a second-hand God. His temple shone with the glorious splendor of the purest gold, the finest tapestries, and the world's most precious gems. Our God desires His children to enjoy abundance and blessing. In this way, others will be drawn to ask, "Just who is this God you serve?" There is a fine line between this perspective and following the Lord only because of what we will receive. Those motivations will certainly surface, and the God who intimately knows our impure hearts will deal with them until they are removed. He does, however, want us to anticipate and embrace the abundant blessings He has stored up for His people.

Ask to see signs. We need to ask God for the eyes to see that the wilderness is ending and to be able to spot the signs of harvest along our path. Just as we can smell fall in the air, feel the brisk onset of winter, and witness the first buds at springtime, so we can sense a change of season in other areas of our lives. Things suddenly begin to change for us, doors begin to open, people begin to seek us out to do those things we have longed to do. When you see these signs, embrace them. Do not, under any circumstances, return to the wilderness mentality saying, "This will probably fall apart too. I wonder what I'm going to have to lose on this part of the journey." This is another land mine we talked about earlier. See the mine for what it is—a mental ploy of your unseen enemy to discourage you before you even take the first step! Rather, mentally and verbally embrace your "new land" and commit to work it, tend it, and mine it. And above all, bless the Lord for the harvest and the abundance.

The land was already occupied. When the Israelites reached the Promised Land, there were entire races of people deeply entrenched there. The occupation of the land, therefore, required hard work and seemingly endless battles. We mistakenly have the picture that they walked over some invisible border and were greeted by an empty land flowing with milk and honey. Nothing could be further from the truth.

Expect battles. Read the books of Joshua and Judges. You will see how many battles the Israelites had to fight in order to claim their inheritance according to God's promise to Abraham. In fact, the current problems in the Middle East trace their roots to this historical time of claiming their territory.

In like manner, when we arrive at our destiny—by that I mean have the certainty within us of what our Creator desires us to be—expect that you will not be welcomed with open arms. If you are to be an actress, and you begin to exercise your God-given right of destiny and become aggressive to take your place among other actors, don't think for a minute they are going to bow down to you and move out of your way!

A word of caution here: I don't think it pleases God to mow other people down just to push ourselves forward. There is a proverb I love: "Do you see a man skillful in his work? He will stand before kings; he will not stand before obscure men" (Prov. 22:29). I believe the proper way we rise to the top is through our art, through the skill acquired in our field along the creative journey.

Settling into your destiny often takes a lifetime. We don't arrive at our final destination overnight, struggle-free. In fact, there may seem to be so many skirmishes along the way, it looks like the wilderness all over again. Again, it's all in maintaining the perspective of taking each day and making the most of it, looking to our Creator for direction, wisdom in how to grow in our art, and ways our lives can enrich others.

Do I believe I'm going to be wildly successful as a writer and producer? Not necessarily. That isn't my mental focus any longer. I am to do what I am called to do each day, and what opens up for me as I move forward on my path. I have learned from a dear friend always to say, "As the Lord wills," for we have no certainties in this life except birth and death.

Complete your task and leave the results to God. Moses was given the special assignment of leading God's people to the Promised Land. He completed his assignment, and yet, if you recall, he never entered the Promised Land himself; he only glimpsed it from afar. Yet Moses fulfilled God's purpose for his life and is called "the friend of God."

One of the sweetest passages in the Scriptures is the end of Deuteronomy, which tells how God led Moses to Mount Nebo, to the top of Pisgah, which is opposite Jericho, and showed him all the land. "So Moses the servant of the Lord died there in the land of Moab, according to the word of the Lord, and he buried him in the valley in the land of Moab...but no man knows the place of his burial to this day" (Deut. 34:5-6). The Lord himself buried His faithful servant. What greater joy could anyone have?

CHAPTER 13

Creative Staying Power

The Scripture is filled with great leaders of faith who achieved their destiny, only to lose it. Saul's kingdom was removed and given to David because of his disobedience and people-pleasing tendencies. Solomon's kingdom rose to tremendous heights, but was ultimately cut short because of his problem with women and subsequent idolatry. "He had seven hundred wives, princesses, and three hundred concubines; and his wives turned away his heart...after other gods; and his heart was not wholly true to the Lord his God" (1 Kings 11:3-4). This principle is not just applicable to the people of God. Nebuchadnezzar spent years out in the wilderness raving like a madman and eating grass like the animals because he set himself up as a god to be worshipped, believing his might and power were responsible for the glory that was Babylon's.

Even when we do experience success, there is always the choice that we make daily: to continue to follow God or turn our backs and go our own way. It is in this period of success that the temptation is so great for turning away. Proverbs says, "Give me neither poverty nor riches; feed me with the food that is needful for me, lest I be full, and deny thee, and say, 'Who is the Lord?' or lest I be poor, and steal, and profane the name of my God" (Prov. 30:8-9).

Keep God's perspective always. One of my favorite passages in all of Scripture is Deuteronomy 8. The historical context in which Deuteronomy was written was that period of time when the Israelites had completed their wilderness wanderings and were poised to enter the Promised Land. God directed Moses to summarize all they had experienced from His perspective, and promised unlimited blessings and divine favor if they followed His directives. In the eighth chapter, Moses described the land lying before them, filled with all manner of provision, abundance, and blessings. "And you shall eat and be full, and you shall bless the Lord your God for the good land he has given you" (Deut. 8:10).

The following verse, however, contains the all-too-human temptation to err: "Beware lest you say in your heart, 'My power and the might of my hand have gotten me this wealth.' You shall remember the Lord your God, for it is he who gives you power to get wealth" (Deut. 8:17-18). This tendency to self-engrandizement is so powerful that I believe it's the reason God purposely tests us so severely. When we truly experience total lack, only then can we be more protected against this puffing up of self. When we undergo the death of a vision, we experience with every part of us our total dependence upon God, because everything we attempt to do in ourselves is blocked. We become utterly helpless in all our self-strivings. During this season, the fear of God becomes permanently lodged in the depth of our souls. Finally, we are given the first glimpse of wisdom: "The fear of God is the beginning of wisdom" (Ps. 111:10).

I recall a lunch meeting I had a few years ago with an entertainment executive who monopolized the entire meeting recounting all of his achievements, how many people owed their successes to his abilities, what wonderful things he was responsible for accomplishing, how the industry was where it was because of his efforts. I couldn't help but cringe inside for I believe that when our mouths declare self-praise and we exalt ourselves for glory and adoration, we set ourselves up for a major fall. Two admonitions are applicable here: "Pride goes before destruction, and a haughty spirit before a fall" (Prov. 16:18); and "Let another praise you, and not your own mouth" (Prov. 27:2).

What happens if we begin to take personal credit for our success and prosperity? Think about Nebuchadnezzar, Saul, and Solomon. "If you forget the Lord your God and go after other gods [i.e., money, fame, recognition, etc.] and serve them and worship them, I solemnly warn you this day that you shall surely perish"

(Deut. 8:19). We have certainly seen leaders come and go, rise and fall, be honored and disgraced, lauded and shamed. It is God alone who raises up leaders and He alone who removes them.

Rewards come through righteousness. The promise of harvest is connected very strongly with the principle of doing the work in a righteous manner. Paul sets forth this principle to the Corinthians: "He who supplies seed to the sower and bread for food will supply and multiply your resources and increase the harvest of your righteousness" (2 Cor. 9:10). This passage contains several promises. First, there is a promise that God will do three things: supply what we need, multiply our resources, and increase the harvest. However, there is a caveat. The work has to be done in righteousness.

Righteousness is a divine attribute. God is totally just, merciful, holy, and righteous. These qualities set Him apart from every other spirit being. The context of the 2 Corinthians passage expands the true meaning of righteousness. "God loves a cheerful giver" (v.7), "He gives to the poor" (v.9), and "You will be enriched in every way for great generosity" (v.11), all refer to God's motivation. His heart is one of outreach to others, helping to lift others up, serving others, and putting others' needs first. Righteousness does not mean personal piety; it is not a call to focus inward. Rather, the attribute is intimately bound together with benevolence and service to others. God's heart is toward the poor, the meek, the humble, and the needy. Thus, His promises of harvest and abundance are tied to the benevolence in our hearts.

Let's be honest. Most of us say, "Lord, if You give me a lot, I'll be sure to give to other people." Wrong. We look at famous philanthropists and their charitable foundations and think, "I would do that too if I had a lot of money." Chances are those resources have been divinely multiplied because that philanthropist had a heart set on helping others. We think that giving comes after the getting, whereas God's dynamic is totally the reverse. We give what we have, then comes the getting.

We creatives are too often striving to reach some imagined pinnacle. It's all we can do to survive ourselves, much less worry about giving to other people. "That will come later," we muse, "after I have gotten where I am supposed to be." In the Sermon on the Mount, Jesus exhorts us not to be anxious about our health, or having enough to eat and drink. He promises that when we "seek first his kingdom and his righteousness, all these things shall be yours as well" (Mt. 6:33). There's that word again: righteousness. What He is saying is that if we have the motivation to help others, serve others, and lift up others less fortunate, then all our needs will be met.

Make it to stage three. There are in essence three primary stages the creative undergoes: 1) the Call; 2) the Character-building; and 3) the Commission. The call is that period of time when we can name our seed and apply the faith necessary to activate it. We commit to doing what we now know in our hearts to do. I like to think of this period as equivalent to the escape from bondage, as the Israelites began their exodus from Egypt. The character-building phase is the wilderness. Frankly, that's where most of us die. We often don't make it through the refinement process. Rather, we get blown apart time and time again in our own self-destructive minefields.

If we persevere, however, and remain faithful in our hearts, then we will arrive at this third phase where we are released into our destinies. This third phase may well be at the end of our lives, when we look at ourselves and say, "What can I possibly accomplish now? I'm too old!" That's precisely the time. Jesus accomplished all He was destined to do in the last three years of His earthly life. That is our model. More can be done in our later years, for only then are we mature enough, hopefully, to have the proper perspective.

Just the other day a potential advertising client called to inquire about what my agency could do for him. Here's what I "heard" in his voice: he was young, in a hurry, and knew it all. I discerned very quickly that he wanted me to give him a tip on how to do everything himself. He was convinced he had researched the

Atlanta broadcast market and wanted to know how to negotiate better rates. I tried to explain that it's a waste of ad dollars to just throw money on a radio station without proper research and planning. He was much too impatient to hear any of this. All he wanted was the best rate. What was the cheapest spot he could purchase? I told him bluntly, "I don't believe I can help you. It sounds to me like you have your mind already made up on which way you want to go." He was taken back somewhat that I wasn't begging for his business. I could tell he was not teachable. He was in a hurry and wanted no part of being educated or led into successful ad campaign management. When we get in a hurry with God, that urgency comes across in endless ways such as self-centered pleas that pass for prayers and setting timelines in our daytimers for God to do something. Almighty God will simply not play our immature game, and waits until our impatience is fully spent.

THE SEVENFOLD FORMULA FOR LIFE-CHANGING CREATIVITY

When all of these separate phases (which we have previously discussed) are in alignment, something magnificent happens: the glory and high-calling of God resonate through our creative giftings and truly impact and change our world.

#1 **The Call**: It is that time when the inspiration of God fills us with the personal sense of our destinies and the Law of Applied Faith is operational.

#2 **The Life Message**: The character-building phase wherein we realize that we have something unique to say. Our lives become a living testimony which tells a story to others: hopefully a story of hope, restoration, and redemption.

#3 **The Skill of the Craft**: The period of time that it takes to perfect our particular skills and giftings, especially those that the Creator desires most to use in the final stage of our realization.

#4 **Favor with God**: God is pleased when the self-centered motivations of our hearts have been refined, when we truly are seeking God's kingdom and His righteousness. Again, arrival at this stage often takes many years.

#5 Favor with Man: For most of us, this stage is difficult to realize. We may know inside what we can do, but there is no way we can convince others to "let us show them what we can do." We have to arrive at the place where we are sought out, where others look at us for skill, leadership, or whatever. It is definitely not a phase we can hurry or buy. No amount of money will secure favor with man, or any of the other stages, for that matter.

#6 The Season: In everything there is a season, and that means a season when "it all comes together" at the right time and the right place.

#7 God's Anointed Blessing: This is the final commissioning stage wherein what we do carries with it the power and strength of the Holy Spirit, who touches lives in ennobling ways.

Notice that when any of these phases is missing or deficient, we will be off-target in what we were destined to be. We can see very clearly how few of us ever arrive at this unique juncture, which is why Jesus' words ring so true: "Many are called, but few are chosen." Through examining ourselves in light of these seven phases, we can make an honest assessment of our journey: see where we are and where we need to experience growth. We should also be encouraged to see how far we have come. We need to take careful note of how the enemy tries to derail us in each of these phases. That's because he knows the power that is able to be released to change our world when these seven phases come into alignment.

THE CALL TO CHANGE YOUR WORLD

We are each uniquely and wonderfully made, with a destiny to grow and multiply and have dominion in our areas of gifting and calling. We have God's promises of strength, provision, protection, and continued blessing, *if* we are willing to pay the price. If we are, then we can change our world with the awesome power of God Himself. That is His heart, for He hears the cries of the needy. What He seeks, though, is vessels willing to commit to the journey. The journey is long. It is hard. Only the strong survive. But remember, God is our strength.

Mine has been a creative as well as a spiritual journey. My desire for this book is that in some way it may help lead you toward your "promised land"...your destiny...to help you break away from your creative bondage, offer words of encouragement as you go through your wilderness, and hold out the promise of harvest, whether in this life or the next.

Endnotes

[1] David Keirsey and Marilyn Bates, *Please Understand Me* (Del Mar, CA: Prometheus Nemesis Book Co., 1979).

[2] Al Ries and Jack Trout, *The 22 Immutable Laws of Marketing* (New York: HarperCollins Publishers, Inc., 1993).

[3] Henry T. Blackaby and Richard Blackaby, *Experiencing God* (Nashville, TN: Broadman & Holman Publishers, 1997), Nov. 2.

[4] Napoleon Hill, *Grow Rich With Peace of Mind* (Greenwich, CT: Fawcett Publications, Inc., 1967), pg. 138.

[5] Ralph Gower, *The New Manners and Customs of Bible Times* (Chicago: Moody Press, 1987).

[6] Ralph Mattson and Arthur Miller, *Finding A Job You Can Love* (Nashville, TN: Thomas Nelson, Inc., 1982).

[7] Napoleon Hill, *Think and Grow Rich* (New York: Ballentine Books, 1960), pg. 32.

[8] Napoleon Hill, *Grow Rich With Peace of Mind*, pg. 150.

[9] *Experiencing God*, Feb. 2.

[10] Lamar Boschman, *The Rebirth of Music* (Shippensburg, PA: Destiny Image Publishers, Inc., 1980), pgs. 3-5.

[11] Leanne Payne, *The Healing Presence* (Grand Rapids, MI: Baker Books, 1989), pg. 192.

[12] John and Paula Sandford, *The Elijah Task* (Tulsa, OK: Victory House, Inc., 1977), pg. 194.

[13] Julia Cameron, *The Artist's Way* (New York: G.P. Putnam's Sons, 1992), pg. 92.

About the Author

CANDACE LONG has worked as a creative for over 30 years. An award-winning songwriter and radio/television producer, she is also the writer of six screenplays and two books. Founder & President of Creative Concepts Advertising, Inc. in Atlanta, she is known for her creative business solutions, hands-on production, and visionary thinking.

In 1994 she founded an entertainment development company to write and produce life-affirming projects for live theatre, television and film. Her projects have attracted the attention of such companies as ABC, NBC, Pax-TV, Hearst Entertainment, Disney, 20th Century Fox, and Universal.

In 2001, she re-staged the World Premiere of her award-winning theatrical musical, *A Time To Dance*. In 2003, she produced an instrumental CD called *Meditation*.

She served as President of Georgia's Women In Film; Vice-Chair/Communications for Women in Film & Television International; and was appointed by Gov. Roy Barnes to serve on the Georgia Film, Video, and Music Advisory Commission.

In 2004, she established a 501(c)(3) organization called Creativity Training Institute and offers seminars, speaking engagements, and workshops for businesses and organizations on a ground-breaking way to activate your creative and gifted people to expand their present level of creativity and reach their God-given potential.

To contact the author for speaking engagements:
Candace Long, Executive Director
Creativity Training Institute
885 Woodstock Road, Suite 430 #337
Roswell, GA 30075-2274
www.creativitytraininginstitute.com